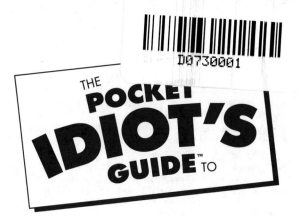

THE
POCKET
IDIOT'S
GUIDE™ TO

Christianity

by Brian Wilson,
adapted by Nancy D. Lewis

ALPHA
A Pearson Education Company

Adapted from the original, published as *Religions of the World: Christianity, First Edition,* by Brian Wilson, published by Pearson Education, Inc., publishing as Prentice Hall, Copyright © 1999 Laurence King Publishing Ltd.

The Pocket Idiot's Guide to Christianity published by Pearson Education, Inc., publishing as Alpha Books, Copyright © 2003, Laurence King Publishing Ltd.

International Standard Book Number: 0-02-864480-8
Library of Congress Catalog Card Number: 2002111666

04 03 02   8 7 6 5 4 3 2 1

Interpretation of the printing code: The rightmost number of the first series of numbers is the year of the book's printing; the rightmost number of the second series of numbers is the number of the book's printing. For example, a printing code of 02-1 shows that the first printing occurred in 2002.

Printed in the United States of America

Note: This publication contains the opinions and ideas of its authors. It is intended to provide helpful and informative material on the subject matter covered. It is sold with the understanding that the authors and publisher are not engaged in rendering professional services in the book. If the reader requires personal assistance or advice, a competent professional should be consulted.

The authors and publisher specifically disclaim any responsibility for any liability, loss, or risk, personal or otherwise, which is incurred as a consequence, directly or indirectly, of the use and application of any of the contents of this book.

For marketing and publicity, please call: 317-581-3722

The publisher offers discounts on this book when ordered in quantity for bulk purchases and special sales.

For sales within the United States, please contact: Corporate and Government Sales, 1-800-382-3419 or corpsales@pearsontechgroup.com

Outside the United States, please contact: International Sales, 317-581-3793 or international@pearsontechgroup.com

Contents

Introduction

This is a short book on a vast topic. During the past two millennia, Christianity has evolved through a myriad of permutations and variations, creating scores of groups and movements, all claiming the appellation of Christian. The goal of this text, therefore, is not to exhaustively document all the possible ways of being Christian. Rather, it is an attempt to introduce you to the sweep of Christian history and to some of the natural mechanisms by which the tradition has diversified and changed over the centuries.

Of course, to do even this in the short space of this book has meant making many difficult choices. Several relevant topics and figures have had to be left to more detailed studies. Nevertheless, I am confident that you, armed with this introduction, will not only possess a good working knowledge of Christianity, but will be in an excellent position to pursue more in-depth studies of this fascinating religious tradition.

Extras

The sidebars in this book offer extra information and help to explain the topics and terms throughout the book. Use these as road signs on the journey to understanding Christianity.

Spread the Word

These boxes define terms familiar to Christianity that are used in the text. Understanding the typical vocabulary and jargon of the religion helps you better understand the general subject when you encounter these terms in another context.

Divine Inspiration

These boxes will be filled with tips about the text to supplement information on the topic at hand.

Bet You Didn't Know

These boxes are extra tidbits of background information that are informative or just plain interesting.

On the Right Path

These boxes provide general guidance about Christianity, which support the materials in the text. They take a topic one step further toward understanding the religion.

Trademarks

All terms mentioned in this book that are known to be or are suspected of being trademarks or service marks have been appropriately capitalized. Alpha Books and Pearson Education, Inc., cannot attest to the accuracy of this information. Use of a term in this book should not be regarded as affecting the validity of any trademark or service mark.

Chapter 1

The Beginnings of the Jesus Movement

In This Chapter

- Yahweh and the Jews
- Theology of the restoration of Israel
- Historical Jesus
- How could the Messiah die?
- From Messiah to Christ

Christianity today is the largest religious tradition in the world, with some 1.8 billion adherents, a remarkable fact considering its origins. Beginning in the first century C.E. and centering on an obscure charismatic Jewish peasant preacher named Jesus of Nazareth, Christianity quickly grew beyond the boundaries of the Land of Israel, and eventually became the established religion of the Roman Empire in the fourth century C.E. From this imperial base and its successors, Christian missionaries fanned out over the next millennium and a half to bring the Christian message to the rest of the world.

Even from its origins, Christianity was not a unified tradition. Christianity, as you shall see, resulted from an amalgamation of elements from many traditions. Jesus was a Jew, and therefore many important themes and ideas were derived from his Jewish heritage. Moreover, Jesus himself was not the founder of the Christian Church. There were many churches in the beginning, founded by many people. Some were Jews, and therefore they shared the Hebraic worldview of Jesus. Others, however, were Greeks, and indeed, one of the most important figures in early Christian history—Paul of Tarsus—was a Jew influenced by Greek ideas.

The Jewish Context

Scholars believe that the ancestors of the Jewish people, the Hebrews, were themselves descendants of the Semitic peoples who invaded Mesopotamia and who founded the city-state of Akkad in the third millennium B.C.E. At some point, probably around 1700 B.C.E., a group of these Mesopotamian Semites reverted to the life of shepherds and migrated out of Mesopotamia southward, eventually settling among another Semitic-language-speaking group, the Canaanites. The majority of these emigrants settled down and began to assimilate large amounts of Canaanite culture. Others, however, continued their nomadic lifestyle and made their way south into Egypt. These were the ancient Hebrews.

Around 1200 B.C.E., the Hebrews returned to the land of the Canaanites, and they attempted to reintegrate themselves into Canaanite society. But the integration would not be easily effected since, during their sojourn in Egypt, they had undergone a startling religious transformation.

The Hebrews were no longer polytheists, worshipers of many gods, but had become monotheists, believers in one god alone. They rejected the polytheism of the indigenous Canaanites. Moreover, the deity of the Hebrews was not a god of a single place, but a deity who traveled with his people, bound to them by a promise or *covenant*.

Spread the Word

A **covenant** is a bond sealed between God and the Jews by which the Jews are promised God's favor in exchange for their fidelity. Christians believe that because of the sacrifices of Jesus, they are successors to the Jews in this bond.

Called Yahweh, the one god promised the Hebrews that he would help them prosper if, in return, they remained faithful by observing a strict code of ethical behavior and performing a set of specific rituals. So important was this religious transformation that the Hebrews took a new name, Israelites, after Jacob Israel, an earlier tribal leader who had been privileged with a direct encounter with Yahweh.

The Israelites became so religiously different from their distant cousins, the Canaanites, that shortly after they entered the Land of Canaan, they entered a period of extended conflict during which the Israelites gradually and violently took control of the land from the Canaanites. During this same period, the Israelites—influenced by the Canaanites and out of military necessity—adopted the institution of kingship. Before this time, the Israelites had been ruled by "judges," who were actually temporary generals or warlords elected by a committee on an ad hoc basis.

> ### Bet You Didn't Know
>
> The office of judge was not hereditary; they were selected by virtue of their charisma, which is a strong and obvious spiritual presence, a sense that the individual is uniquely gifted by God to hold a special role. It is a person who is uncommonly spiritually attractive to others, a natural-born leader.

Shortly after the creation of the Israelite monarchy in the year 1000 B.C.E., King David successfully unified the tribes and created a capital centered in the old Canaanite city of Jerusalem. Here the Israelites developed a highly sophisticated center of worship, complete with a magnificent temple, a professional priesthood, a complex *liturgy*, massive animal sacrifices, and annual festivals for which the entire population of the countryside would make a pilgrimage to Jerusalem.

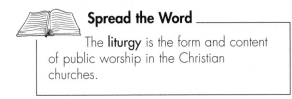

Spread the Word _____

The **liturgy** is the form and content of public worship in the Christian churches.

It was during this period that the collection of sacred scriptures, which would eventually become the Hebrew Bible (called the Old Testament by Christians), began to take shape. Eventually, David and his son Solomon would create an Israelite empire that extended from Mesopotamia to Egypt.

The Culture Clash Begins

The monarchy of David and Solomon represented the high-water mark of Israelite civilization. From the moment of Solomon's death, the Israelites suffered a series of political and military setbacks that would ultimately lead to the complete loss of autonomy of the Land of Israel. A series of colonial overlords controlled the land for most of the first millennium B.C.E.: first the Assyrians, next the Babylonians and Persians, then the Greeks, and finally, in 63 B.C.E., the Romans, who absorbed the land into the burgeoning Roman Empire. The Romans referred to the Land of Israel as the province of Judea and to the people who lived there as Jews.

The misfortunes of this period led to a wholesale reevaluation of Israelite theology, often by people called *prophets*. Isaiah, an eighth-century religious teacher and prophet attached to the Jerusalem temple, convinced his listeners that these misfortunes signified God's displeasure with the Israelites, and that they were on the road to disaster. Isaiah, however, balanced this prophecy of impending doom with another of great hope. At one point, Isaiah announced that in time there would appear a woman of the line of David who would give birth to a son who would save Israel. It is not known to whom Isaiah was referring, but the idea of a future king of the line of David, one who would be anointed with the oil of royalty—a messiah—would from then on become an enduring part of Jewish belief.

Spread the Word

Prophets are religious reformers who legitimate their reformist goals by claiming to speak for God.

Diaspora and Their Synagogues

During this period, Jews increasingly began to emigrate out of the Land of Israel, either for political or economic reasons. This led to the creation of large overseas Jewish communities, collectively called the Diaspora (Greek for "dispersion"). To serve the religious needs of these overseas Jews, there developed local centers of religious observance and instruction, institutionalized as the synagogue (Greek for "assembly"). In time, synagogues would become commonplace in the Land of Israel itself.

Many overseas Jews during this period came to absorb a great deal of Greek and Roman culture, and this influence was felt in the Land of Israel. The rich and educated among the Jews became bilingual, speaking Greek; in time, the Hebrew Bible was translated into Greek (the so-called *Septuagint*).

Sadducees and Pharisees (and Zealots)

Not all Jews in Judea, however, were enthusiastic about this inundation of Greek and Roman culture, nor were many content with Roman rule. The Sadducees, for example, were the elite priestly families who were intensely concerned with the continuation of temple ritual, and therefore they were distrustful of foreign cultural influences in the land.

Another religious party was the Pharisees, who were essentially the synagogue rabbis or teachers. Like the Sadducees, the Pharisees were concerned with foreign cultural influences, although they were less interested in temple ritual than the Sadducees. Instead, they were more interested in individual ritual purity—purity that could only be maintained through strict adherence to the dietary and other "lifestyle" laws found in the Hebrew Bible.

The Pharisees therefore saw the laxity of Greco-Roman culture as a threat to such purity. Moreover, there also developed within the ranks of the Pharisees a small group committed to the violent overthrow of Roman rule; these were known as the Zealots. The Zealots believed that their armed resistance to the Romans was a necessary step toward ushering in the days of the messiah, the Davidic king who would rid the Land of Israel of all foreign influences and reestablish the Israelite kingdom forever.

Bet You Didn't Know _____

The Zealots in Judea during the first century C.E. were where the terms "religious zealot" and "fanatic" first became associated. Many times people refer to individuals who reign terror or bring harm to others—based on their personal belief that their god or leader told them their actions are just—as religious zealots.

Miracle Workers and Magicians

Not all such movements were as well defined as these, however, especially in rural areas of the Land of Israel. The Judean countryside played host to a swarm of itinerant miracle workers and magicians, healers and holy men, spiritual charlatans, and charismatic rabble-rousers.

During the early first century C.E., for example, a man named Eleazer exorcised demons from possessed people; another named Onias claimed to command the forces of nature at will; a third, Hanina ben Dosa of Galilee, practiced long-distance spiritual healing; and a fourth named Theudas claimed to work miracles in the name of God.

Some of these men and women even claimed that they were the messiah or the messiah's herald, and, as they drifted in and out of the small towns and villages of Judea, some would occasionally attract a small following, not to mention the watchful eyes of the local authorities. Few of these movements lasted for long, but they did help to encourage a ravaged peasant population starved for hope, both spiritual and political, and for this reason they continually reappeared. It was into this world that Jesus was born and raised.

The Jesus We Know Of

Jesus himself left no writings, no autobiography, and very little of what he actually said can be recovered with any historical confidence. The Christian scriptures, including the four biographies of Jesus called the Gospels, were written sometime after Jesus' death. Our modern picture of Jesus is therefore based on analysis of these documents and putting them into context with first-century Judaism.

Current scholarship surmises that Jesus was probably born in lower Galilee sometime around 6 to 4 B.C.E. His family, poor but not destitute, eked out a living as village artisans as did so many other Mediterranean peasants of their day. Jesus was probably trained in his father's work, carpentry, but likely had little or no formal education. He probably did, however, attend the local synagogue and gained there at least an oral familiarity with the Hebrew scriptures and the demands of Pharisaic Judaism. Moreover, Jesus, like his neighbors, would have been familiar with the itinerant world of healers, exorcists, and petty prophets who passed through the Galilean countryside.

At some point in his life, Jesus was attracted to the teachings of one such preacher named John. It is not clear from the historical record where John came from, or what his background was. By the time Jesus encountered him, he was preaching on the banks of the Jordan River, a day's walk from Jesus' hometown of Nazareth. There, John was preaching the old message of the prophets, placing special emphasis on the imminent end of the current sinful world and the establishment of God's kingdom in a new one. Those who wished to survive the transition from this corrupt world to the *Kingdom of God*, John taught, must undergo the ancient Jewish purification ritual of *baptism*. Jesus, it seems, accepted John's message and John's baptism.

As with so many other wandering charismatics of the day, John attracted the close scrutiny of the Roman authorities who saw such preaching as politically subversive. John the Baptist was quickly arrested and executed. In the wake of John's death, Jesus embarked on his own preaching career. Jesus, however, seems to have subtly altered John's message, implying that the kingdom of God had already been established on Earth.

Spread the Word _____

The **Kingdom of God** is considered by Christians to be the rule of God on Earth, which is now manifested in the churches, but which will ultimately be universal at the end of time. **Baptism** is the Christian ritual of initiation by which a person is spiritually purified through contact with water. Christians adopted the practice in imitation of Jesus' baptism by John at the River Jordan, as depicted in the Gospels.

As proof of the kingdom, Jesus offered up miracles of healing and exorcism. As a consequence of the kingdom, Jesus encouraged his listeners to move toward a social equality, a breaking down of the hierarchies that divided people from one another. As awkward as this message was—especially in the highly stratified and patriarchal culture of Ancient Israel—Jesus did manage to attract a group of followers who accompanied him as he traveled from village to village spreading his message.

It is not known whether Jesus had, at this point, come to the notice of the political authorities as John had. Jesus himself, however, sealed his fate when he decided to take his message to the very religious, political heart of the Land of Israel—Jerusalem.

Jerusalem was crowded with people during the festival seasons, and the temple was an excellent place for Jesus to address an audience larger than any he could find in the countryside. Thus, sometime before *Passover*, Jesus and his followers entered the city, and Jesus began preaching within the temple precincts.

Either because of the nature of his message, or because of some incident in the temple, or perhaps both, Jesus quickly came to the attention of the religious and political authorities of the city. Just as quickly, and probably quite casually, Jesus was executed by the Romans through the common means of crucifixion. This occurred sometime around 33 C.E.

> **Spread the Word**
>
> **Passover** is the annual celebration, in Judaism, of the Ancient Hebrews' escape from slavery in Egypt.

The Problem with the Crucified Messiah

Exactly what happened immediately in the wake of Jesus' death cannot be known with any historical certainty. Perhaps the first response of Jesus' followers was disbelief, followed by headlong flight from Jerusalem.

Despite the unceremonious collapse of Jesus' movement, however, at least a small group of his followers remained in contact with each other. Moreover, the charisma of Jesus continued to exercise a grip over the imaginations of his followers as they struggled to come to terms with his violent and ignominious death on the cross.

For some, Jesus was undoubtedly the messiah. And yet, if Jesus were messiah, how could he die? The only possible answer to this question was that he never died, or that if he died, then he was resurrected from the dead. Jesus, therefore, was alive, and, as messiah, would soon return to usher in the kingdom of God of which he had spoken.

Jesus' death was one great *atonement* for the sins of Israel, a massive, all-encompassing sacrifice. Moreover, while Jesus served as a symbol of the redemption of Israel, he was also an individual. In this way, his death and resurrection simultaneously held the promise of individual *salvation* from death as well.

Spread the Word

Atonement is the reconciliation of God with humankind. **Salvation** is the achievement of eternal life.

With the confidence of this conviction, some of Jesus' followers returned to Jerusalem and began to preach Jesus' message (though more cautiously), as well as the news of his resurrection. For these *apostles*, the good news of Jesus was aimed at Jews exclusively, as it concerned the redemption of Israel. Moreover, the first members of the movement quite naturally saw themselves as Jews before all else, and thus they continued to practice the laws as set down in the Hebrew Bible, including temple worship. At this point, therefore, the "Jesus movement" could quite properly be seen as a sect within Judaism.

> **Spread the Word** _____
>
>   Specifically, an **apostle** refers to
> one of the followers of Jesus who was cho-
> sen to preach the Gospel; generally, it
> refers to any person who engages in a
> Christian mission.

The Gentiles' Mission

From the centers in both Jerusalem and Galilee, the
Jesus movement began to send out emissaries to
bring the good news to synagogues, both in Israel
and in the Diaspora. Quite possibly, these emissaries
presented oral versions of Jesus' biography as well
as examples of his sayings to their synagogue audiences. This had two major impacts on the development of the tradition.

First, the message of Jesus' messiahship was still
seen as inherently political, and although it interested some Jews, many synagogue authorities were
quick to persecute these missionaries out of fear of
Roman retribution. Among the new missionaries,
this quickly inspired a negative attitude toward the
synagogue authorities and, eventually, toward traditional Judaism itself.

The second major impact of the mission to the synagogues was that it was the conduit by which the
message of Jesus began to reach the Hellenic or
Greek-speaking world and to attract non-Jewish
("Gentile") followers. Such Gentile followers of

Jesus were called Christians, after the word *christos* (Greek for "anointed one" or "messiah").

Paul of Tarsus

The mission to the Gentiles, however, only really began to expand rapidly with the appearance of Paul of Tarsus (d. c. 65 C.E.). Paul, who never met Jesus, was nevertheless the most successful missionary of the early Jesus movement. Considering his early life, Paul's championing of the movement seems highly unlikely, for although he was born and raised in the Diaspora, Paul was also raised a strict Pharisee and his sympathies at first lay with the synagogue authorities. Indeed, by Paul's own admission, he was probably one of the most energetic persecutors of the missionaries of the Jesus movement. However, according to his own words, Paul had undergone a powerful conversion experience while traveling to Damascus. From then on, Paul became an ardent promoter of Jesus' messiahship throughout the Diaspora.

Having been raised in the Diaspora and being at home in Hellenic culture, Paul was enthusiastic about the growing Gentile presence among the newly organized Christian congregations of Asia Minor. He was anxious to facilitate their initiation into the movement. Paul decided that, for Gentiles, conversion to Judaism was not necessary. This distressed the Jerusalem church, whose missionaries did require such a conversion to become a Christian. This created friction between the Jerusalem church and Paul's mission.

At length, Paul, fearing for the unity of the Jesus movement, journeyed to Jerusalem to make his peace with the Jewish-Christian church there. In the year 48 C.E., an Apostolic Council was convened. There, it was decided that the Jewish Christians would accept the conversion of Gentiles, if Paul's Diaspora congregations would accept the primacy of the Jerusalem church and contribute to its financial support. Satisfied with this arrangement, Paul returned to his missionary labors in Asia Minor, and then extended his work into mainland Greece.

Soon, however, it became clear to Paul that the Jewish-Christian missions from Jerusalem were continuing to undermine his own mission by insisting that Gentile Christians follow the ritual prescriptions of the Hebrew Bible. In response, Paul was forced to explicitly reject these ritual prescriptions, maintaining that the covenant God previously made with Israel had been replaced by a new covenant with the Gentiles. Indeed, Paul argued that it was the Gentiles who in time would bring Israel back to God. Paul formulated a "Gentile-friendly" theology in which salvation (called justification by Paul) was achieved not by the ritual prescriptions of the Hebrew Bible, but as a free gift of grace from God. Grace, according to Paul, could not be earned by ritual work, but only through faith in the truth of God and Jesus.

Judea Becomes Palestine

Ultimately, the rivalry between Paul's Gentile church and the Jewish Christians at Jerusalem was decided not on theological grounds, but by the rush of political events. In the year 66 C.E., the Jews of Jerusalem revolted against Roman rule, and they even managed to expel the Roman procurator from the city. At first, the Romans did not take this revolt too seriously, but it soon spread to the rest of Judea.

On the Right Path

In Christian theology, justification is the reconciliation of one's will with the will of God, leading to salvation; grace is God's love and assistance freely given to Christian believers without which salvation would not be possible.

The following year, the Roman general Titus ruthlessly reduced the countryside to submission and besieged Jerusalem itself. The city fell a year later. All Jews were summarily expelled from the city, the temple was destroyed a second time, and Judea was renamed Palestine.

The Jewish-Christian church of Jerusalem fled north into the countryside, where it survived for several generations. However, without its symbolic home of Jerusalem, the Jewish-Christian church gradually faded from historical view. The fate of the Christian tradition now lay largely in the hands of the Gentile churches.

The Least You Need to Know

- The deity of the monotheist Hebrews was not a god of a single place, but one who traveled with his people, bound to them by a promise or covenant.

- The prophet Isaiah announced that in time there would appear a woman of the line of King David who would give birth to a son who would save Israel.

- Large overseas Jewish communities were collectively called the Diaspora; to serve their religious needs, synagogues were developed as local centers of religious observance and instruction.

- The Sadducees were the elite priestly families concerned with the continuation of temple ritual and didn't trust foreign cultural influences; the Pharisees were the rabbis and teachers at the synagogues; the Zealots (a group within the Pharisees) believed that their armed resistance to the Romans was a necessary step toward ushering in the days of the messiah.

- Our modern picture of Jesus is based on analysis of the Scriptures and Gospels, as well as putting them into context with first-century Judaism.

- The only possible answer to why Jesus (the messiah) could possibly die was that he never did, or that if he died, then he was resurrected from the dead.

Christianity from the First Century to Late Antiquity

In This Chapter

- Matthew, Mark, Luke, and John
- Christianity's links with Judaism
- Partaking of Eucharist and Baptism
- Christianity becomes popular
- Hebraic, Greek, and Gnostic worldviews
- The Christian Canon is fixed

The Greek or Hellenic worldview came to play an increasingly important role in the formation of the Christian tradition. Thus, as Christianity emerged in the last centuries of Late Antiquity (from c. 1200 B.C.E. to c. 400 C.E.), it already embodied a diversity of cultural and social elements. In this chapter, we trace the historical coming together of these elements.

The Look-Alike Gospels

The written Gospels best illustrate the degree to which Christianity had become a Greek phenomenon by the last third of the first century C.E. The story of Jesus' life and death had circulated orally among the Christian congregations since the first years of the movement, but the earliest existing written versions, dating from the decade of 70 C.E., were produced exclusively in Greek. Moreover, these biographies of Jesus were largely written to appeal to Gentile audiences.

> **Bet You Didn't Know**
>
> The Gospel of Mark (c. 70 C.E.) par-
> allels Jesus' death with the destruction of
> the temple of Jerusalem, as if to say that the
> era ushered in by Jesus' death marked the
> end of Judaism and the extension of God's
> covenant to the Gentile world. Essentially,
> this was Paul of Tarsus's message (see
> Chapter 1), although it was now delivered
> in a dramatically effective way by incorpo-
> rating it symbolically into the story of Jesus.

The slightly later Gospels of Matthew and Luke (both c. 79 C.E.) continued this anti-Jewish contro-versy. Indeed, the Gospels of Matthew and Luke were probably influenced by Mark (and perhaps another version of the Gospel that is no longer in existence). Due to this dependence, the Gospels of Mark, Matthew, and Luke are often referred to as the synoptic or "look-alike" Gospels.

Matthew and Luke, however, emphatically preached that Christianity was the fulfillment of Judaism, not a completely new tradition.

Why Christianity Remained Linked with Judaism

Christianity had to be considered the fulfillment of Judaism for two reasons. First, Matthew and Luke carefully constructed their stories so that events in Jesus' life could be seen as fulfillments of the messianic prophecies as recorded in the Hebrew Bible. If they had rejected Judaism completely, they would have been forced to reject the validity of the Jewish scriptures, and thus the proof of Jesus' messiahship.

The second reason for maintaining the link to Judaism was a matter of status within Roman society. By the time of the writing of these two Gospels (Matthew and Luke), many Christian congregations had been established for several decades and had achieved a certain level of stability. Nevertheless, as a "new religion" within the Roman Empire, Christianity did not enjoy any of the legal protections accorded to those traditions, such as Judaism, which were recognized by the Romans as "ancient traditions."

The Roman state was founded on the belief in the old Roman gods and goddesses, and while new religions in and of themselves were not perceived as threatening to the state, those new religions that demanded an exclusive allegiance were. Such a religion was Christianity, and, therefore, Christian congregations were frequently the target of harassment and persecution by the Roman authorities.

By maintaining the connection to Judaism, and indeed, by claiming that Christianity was the only legitimate form of Judaism, the Gospel writers hoped to cloak Christianity in the legal mantle of an "ancient tradition." In the end, this strategy was of limited value, and it was largely the dynamic growth of Christianity that allowed the tradition to survive into the second century C.E.

Early Church Order

Throughout the second and third centuries C.E., Christianity grew rapidly, spreading from the eastern end of the Mediterranean basin—Palestine and Asia Minor—to the western end—Spain and North Africa. Significant centers of Christians could be found in almost all the major cities of the Roman Empire. Rome itself hosted three separate congregations by the middle of the second century.

The growth of Christianity was due to a variety of factors, of course, but one major factor was that, unlike many of the other new religions of the Empire, the Christian churches maintained an egalitarian ethic, welcoming not only the elite, but also socially lower stature people such as women and slaves. Moreover, while Christian promises of salvation offered security for the next life, the churches' emphasis on charity offered some small amount of social security in this life—a key draw in an Empire where the majority of people lived below the poverty line.

Despite their rapid growth, the Christian churches soon began to exhibit a more or less uniform institutional structure. As it became increasingly clear that the Second Coming of Jesus the Messiah was to be in the far-distant future, the urgent *apocalypticism* of the early decades was replaced by a culture of patient waiting.

Spread the Word

Apocalypticism is the belief in the imminent end of the world; in Christianity, this belief is coupled with the expectation of the Second Coming of Jesus.

Individual congregations began to develop ways of surviving for the long term and for passing the Christian tradition from generation to generation. Individual churches often came to be organized around a threefold hierarchy of offices:

- Bishops
- Presbyters
- Deacons

The highest office was that of bishop, the official responsible for the diocese (territorial jurisdiction) in the Roman Catholic, Eastern Orthodox, Anglican, and other Episcopal churches (derived from the Greek word *episkopos* or "overseer"). The bishop formed the moral center of the congregation and the principal mediator between people and God. Indeed, in the early years, the bishop was the only one who could administer baptism and the *Eucharist.*

 Spread the Word _____

The **Eucharist** is the sacrament of consecrated bread and wine, recreating the last meal partaken by Jesus with his disciples before his crucifixion.

The bishop was aided by a body of elders, or presbyters, in Greek, which is where the word "priest" originated. In addition to helping the bishop in his ritual tasks, the presbyters were charged with the decision-making and financial affairs of the congregation. They also had an important say in who was to be admitted to fellowship in the Church.

Last, there developed the office of deacon (Greek for "servant"). The deacons had a number of important functions. They instructed those wishing membership in the congregation and made sure they were ready for admission to the Church. The deacons also administered charity to the poor, widows, and orphans of the congregation.

Christian Rites and Services

During the first and early second centuries, ritual within the Church remained very simple. Because Christianity was not yet a legal religion, its rites had to be practiced with discretion. Thus, the early Christians were forced to confine their services to private homes or occasionally cemeteries and tombs.

Bet You Didn't Know _____

Christian church services were most often held on Sunday, not only to commemorate Jesus' resurrection on that day, but also to differentiate Christian services from synagogue services (which were on Saturday).

Early Christian services were typically in two parts. The first part consisted of the bishop reading portions from one of the traditional lives of Jesus then in circulation, and next, preaching a sermon to elaborate and explain it. At this point, all in the audience who were not baptized were asked to leave, in order for the second part of the service to proceed. In the early Church, membership was divided between unbaptized *catechumens* and the baptized full members of the congregation. Only those who were full members were allowed to witness and participate in the next ritual, the Eucharist (Greek for "thanksgiving").

> ### Spread the Word
>
> **Catechumens** were people in training for admission to the Church. Because they weren't baptized, they were only allowed to witness the first part of the Mass and were dismissed before the Eucharist.

Eucharist

The Eucharist was, and for many Christians still remains, the central symbol of Christianity, for it recreates the last meal, perhaps the Passover meal, partaken by Jesus and his disciples before his crucifixion. To recreate this meal, the deacons would bring the bishop a loaf of bread and chalice of wine to symbolize the elements of that last meal. The bishop would bless the bread and the wine, and they were then passed around to the baptized to eat and drink.

Even in this simple form, the Eucharist provided baptized members with a powerful experience of Jesus' presence—an experience notable for its awe-inspiring solemnity. It was thus zealously guarded from the unprepared, the uninitiated, or the unworthy. Once the Eucharist had been celebrated, an actual full-scale meal, the *agape* or "love feast," followed, and to this both the baptized and the catechumens were welcome. Unlike the awesome emotions occasioned by the Eucharist, however, this meal emphasized warm fellowship and good cheer. Over the years, though, the festivities of the agape came to be regarded as unseemly and not in keeping with the solemnity of the Eucharist. Slowly, it passed out of common use, leaving only the proper form of the Eucharist.

Spread the Word

An **agape** is a communal meal that was commonly celebrated by early Christians as part of the Eucharist.

Baptism

Baptism, of course, was the second important ritual of the early Church, and it was adopted in imitation of Jesus' baptism by John at the River Jordan, as depicted in the Gospels. In the early churches, baptism was performed only on adults, as it could be received only after passing through a period of doctrinal instruction (the catechumenate). The decision to admit the catechumen, however, was not automatic, but depended on the agreement of the entire congregation.

Once a collective decision had been reached, the catechumen normally waited for the Easter season to actually undergo the rite, since it was during this period that the bishop, the only one who could perform baptisms, would visit each congregation. In time, though, as the number of congregations grew, it became obvious that the bishop could no longer conveniently travel to all his congregations. Thus the twin duties of celebrating the Eucharist and performing baptisms eventually fell to the presbyters (priests), who were specially consecrated for these tasks through a third ritual, priestly *ordination*.

Spread the Word _____

Ordination is the set of rituals by which individuals are admitted to the priesthood or ministry.

Women's Roles (or Lack Thereof)

The evolving role of women in the Church during Late Antiquity is also an indication of the growing institutionalization of Christianity during the period of the second and third centuries. In the beginning, women were free to play an active part in the formation of churches. The Gospels report that Jesus had both male and female followers, and that much of Jesus' financial support came from women. In Paul's letters, women appear as active missionaries; some were even given the title "apostle" by Paul.

Women owned many of the house churches where early Christian groups met, and they often acted as financial patrons of early congregations. In terms of official roles, women served as deaconesses, instructing female catechumens and administering poor relief. Others were recognized as prophets within their congregations, although there seems to be little evidence that women were widely ordained as priests.

In time, however, for a couple of reasons, the roles of women gradually became severely restricted in Christianity. First, as Christianity became better established in the Empire, it became more conservative. Church leaders were anxious to present the faith not as a revolutionary force, but as a preserver of the family values and domestic order so important to Roman culture. This meant, of course, forcing women back into a more submissive posture and back to the traditional roles of wife and mother.

Bet You Didn't Know

By eventually banning divorce and second marriage and by prohibiting contraception and abortion, the emerging Orthodox Church came to impose far greater restrictions on women's lives than did the surrounding Roman culture.

The second reason women's roles were circumscribed was that women were then enjoying higher leadership roles (including ordination) in congregations deemed heretical (guilty of heresy, which were doctrines and beliefs that departed from orthodox teaching) by the majority of the Church. In order to distance themselves from these groups, the Church made the complete subordination of women a badge of orthodoxy, i.e., "correct belief."

Popular Christianity in Late Antiquity

In addition to formal church services, early Christians also developed a variety of informal or "popular" practices. Many such practices were highly syncretic in nature—that is, they blended elements of pagan religious practice with Christian practice. Nowhere can this be better seen than in the development of the cult of saints and martyrs.

With the persecutions of the second and third centuries, the history of Christianity came to be filled with the heroic stories of those who willingly died for their faith. Such people came to be called martyrs, a term derived from the Greek word *martus*, "to witness or testify." As with pagan heroes, the tombs and burial places of the Christian martyrs soon attracted popular devotion. Special anniversary feasts were celebrated at the tombs of local martyrs, and contact with a martyr's tomb was believed to bring about healing and the exorcism of demons.

In response to such beliefs, the Christian churches gradually developed a far-reaching theology accounting for the power of martyrs. Martyrdom, it was taught, was a perfect demonstration of one's faith in the saving power of Jesus, and, because of this, martyrs were rewarded by immediate entrance into heaven. Martyrs did not, as ordinary Christians do, have to wait for the general resurrection at the end of time to enjoy the presence of God. For this reason, martyrs were believed to be in a position to act as mediators between God and human beings still living on Earth.

Prayers addressed to the martyrs were seen as the most effective way to influence God's will, and a martyr's earthly remains, called relics, were seen as objects containing a superabundance of spiritual power.

Over the centuries, the theology of the intercession of martyrs was extended to people who were considered to have lived holy lives, but who did not necessarily die a martyr's death. Called saints (from the Latin word *sanctus*, meaning "holy"), such people were thought to have the same intercessory powers after death as do martyrs. Their tombs, too, began to attract the same kind of cultic devotion and for the same reasons.

The relics of the saints were considered as powerful as the relics of the martyrs, and the trade or theft of such relics were frequent occurrences. The cult of saints and martyrs became so important in the life of the Church that the rediscovery of the resting places of "forgotten" saints and martyrs in towns and cities hitherto without a saint's tomb was commonplace. Usually the location was revealed through a dream or a vision, and once discovered, the remains were removed to a more suitable location, often a pagan shrine converted to Christian usage. In this way, many of the old local pagan gods became assimilated with Christian saints.

On the Right Path

The veneration of icons is an extremely old practice in Eastern Orthodoxy. Early Christians believed that pictures of Jesus and Mary, the angels, saints, and martyrs had special powers of intercession and protection. Typically, icons were created in colorful mosaics or on painted wooden panels, always with materials blessed by a priest. So strong did the veneration of icons become in the Christian East, that the Byzantine emperor Leo III, fearing idolatry, launched a vigorous attack on the practice in the eighth century. This polarized Eastern Christianity into two camps: Iconoclasts (those who rejected icons) and Iconodules (those who accepted them). In the end, the Iconodules prevailed, arguing that to reject icons was to reject the incarnation of Jesus himself, since both were material copies of spiritual beings. Since that time, no Orthodox church would be without its icons, and icons continue to be very popular as aids in domestic worship.

Hebraic vs. Greek Worldviews in Christian Apologetics

Meanwhile, another, albeit more self-conscious, type of "religious tradition blending" was occurring in the Christian world. As Christianity established a higher profile, Christian thinkers were challenged to give Christianity the kind of intellectual legitimacy enjoyed by Greek philosophy. Such Christian thinkers were called *apologists*, a title derived from the Greek word for "defense."

Spread the Word

The Christian **apologists** were a group of theologians from the Ancient period who sought to reinterpret the Christian message in light of Greek philosophy.

For the most part, their work consisted of reinterpreting the Christian message in light of the vastly different theological and cosmological assumptions of the larger Greek world, mainly those derived from the writings of Plato (c. 427–347 B.C.E.), which went by the name of *Neoplatonism* ("new Platonism"). This task was not as easy as it sounds, and Christianity would forever be changed by this attempt at philosophical synthesis.

Spread the Word

Neoplatonism is the concept that conceives of the world as having come from an ultimate being with whom the soul is capable of being reunited.

Hebraic Worldview

Christianity emerged from a Jewish environment, and its early philosophy was built on the assumptions of the Hebraic worldview. Worldviews arise because most human beings have an instinctual need to know their place—both physically and metaphorically—in the cosmos. While worldviews cannot be summed up in a series of simple propositions, two of the outstanding elements of the Hebraic worldview can be indicated, nevertheless:

> The first element is theological: For the Jews, God was usually conceived of as wholly separate from humanity. Human beings may have been created in the likeness of God, but this in itself did not intrude on the permanent transcendence of God.

> The second element is cosmological: Creation was good. No matter how much evil may inhabit it, the material world was and forever would be a gift from God and therefore a boon to humankind.

These two ideas formed the intellectual background of Jewish and early Christian thought. Indeed, for early Christians, the momentousness of Jesus' sacrifice was not only that God became flesh and then allowed the flesh to be killed, but that God also sacrificed his transcendence—if only briefly—in order to do it. Once Christianity entered the Greek world, however, it found itself in a philosophical environment in which these two propositions were reversed.

Greek Worldview

Many Greeks believed that human beings were of a mixed spiritual and material nature. The human soul was spiritual and therefore directly connected in some way to the transcendent source of all souls, called "the One" by some, "God" by others. Because of this connection, the human soul naturally yearned for reunion with God, although many souls remained ignorant of the true nature of this yearning since they were locked in a material body.

Indeed, for Neoplatonists, the material world was something to be escaped, and they therefore looked upon the world either with indifference or with outright hostility. Ideally, for the Neoplatonist, life would be spent in a fierce *asceticism* so as to better enable the soul to concentrate its mystical efforts to reunite with God.

 Spread the Word _____

> **Asceticism** is when an individual practices strict self-denial in order to measure their spiritual discipline. For example, individuals will go for long periods of time without eating or sleeping.

The Greek worldview was pervasive in the Ancient world, and some of its concepts very quickly found their way into Christian discourse. Paul, for example, uses the language of Greek philosophy in some of his letters to the churches. Moreover, the Gospel of John, written sometime after 96 C.E., is explicit in this Hellenic influence, and employs Neoplatonic technical vocabulary.

Some Christian apologists, such as Tertullian (c. 160–225), resisted this shift toward Neoplatonism, while others, such as Justin Martyr (c. 100–165), strove mightily to harmonize the two worldviews within a Christian framework. The two worldviews, however, were essentially irreconcilable.

> ### On the Right Path
>
> Christianity saw the recognition of the eternal gulf between people and God, between material and spiritual, as essential for maintaining the covenant with God; indeed, only by recognizing God's transcendence through action in the material world is salvation even possible. Neoplatonic Christianity, on the other hand, collapsed the distance between God and people, making God immanent in the human soul and seeing the material world as a dangerous impediment.

Gnostic Worldview

Both brands of Christianity had their supporters, and very quickly, schismatic movements began to appear. One such movement, a movement that competed very successfully for a time with Orthodox Christianity, was Christian Gnosticism. The term Gnosticism comes from the word "gnosis," meaning knowledge, and, in this case, special knowledge revealed to a very few.

Gnosticism probably originated before Christianity and represented a fusion of Jewish, Persian, and Greek ideas. Like Neoplatonists, Gnostics sharply separated the material world from the spiritual world. Matter, the Gnostics taught, was evil, and indeed creation was the handiwork not of God, but of a lesser deity, the "demiurge."

According to Christian Gnostics, the importance of Jesus was that he brought secret knowledge (*gnosis*), knowledge that could free the human soul from the material world and enable it to achieve immortality. Further, according to the Christian Gnostics, this secret knowledge had been passed on through a series of specific Gnostic teachers and could only be imparted to an exclusive spiritual elite. Gnostics taught that Jesus had come not as a sacrifice for all humanity, but to bring special knowledge for an elite few. Indeed, considering its popularity, per- haps the only reason that Christian Gnosticism did not overtake Orthodox Christianity was the fact that its growth was checked by its exclusivity.

The Rise of Monasticism

In time, Christian Orthodoxy was forced to adopt a more creative and accommodative attitude toward the Greek worldview. This can clearly be seen in the Orthodox Christian response to the rise of monasticism. Monastics (or "monks") were people who sought to live a more pure Christian life by withdrawing from society and the sensual world, to pursue a life of contemplation. Clearly influenced by a Neoplatonic ethic of asceticism, monasticism quickly spread from Egypt, where it arose in the third century C.E., to Palestine and Asia Minor by the fourth century C.E.

Orthodox Christians looked upon the movement with some concern, as monks typically rejected the authority and practices of the church as part and parcel with their larger rejection of the world. Instead of attacking this practice as they did Gnosticism, however, Orthodox Christian authorities sought to co-opt the movement. The Orthodox bishop Athanasius (c. 296–373), for example, wrote a biography of one of the most famous early monks, Anthony of Egypt (d. 356). In this biography, the figure of Anthony was recast as rigidly orthodox in his beliefs, despite his asceticism.

The Life of Anthony thus provided a model for the ideal Orthodox monk. Later, another bishop, Basil the Great (c. 330–379), explicitly codified the lifestyle for an Orthodox monk living communally in a monastery. The Rule of Basil stressed a balance blending of a life of asceticism with a life of service to the church and community. In some cases, monasteries began offering medical services and poor relief, and later, they became centers of scholarship, and training grounds for bishops and missionaries of Orthodox Christianity.

The Fixing of the Christian Canon

Meanwhile, the conflict between the Hebraic and Greek worldviews had another important impact on the developing tradition, as it ultimately led to the creation of a fixed list (or canon) of documents by Orthodox Christianity. The debate over which documents Christians should be reading was a response to the rise in the early second century of a schismatic Christian movement called Marcionism.

Marcion (d. c. 160) was a wealthy shipbuilder from Asia Minor who migrated to Rome specifically to join the Christian Church there. Around 140 C.E., Marcion fell out with the rest of the congregation and formed a congregation of his own. The tensions came about because Marcion denied that the god of the Hebrew Bible and the god of the Gospels were the same god. The god of the Hebrew Bible, Marcion argued, was a vengeful, angry god, whereas the god of Jesus was a god of light and love.

Marcion, influenced by the Gnostics, associated the god of the Hebrew Bible with the demiurge (from the Gnostic worldview) and the god of Jesus with the Platonic One. Because of this, Marcion taught his followers that the Hebrew Bible should be abandoned as an authoritative text and that all documents now in the Christian tradition that treated the Hebrew Bible as authoritative should be abandoned. Marcion's canon, therefore, included only the Gospel of Luke and the letters of Paul, and even in these documents, Marcion edited out passages in which the Hebrew Bible was mentioned in a positive light.

For the Orthodox Church, this was unacceptable. One of the proofs of Jesus' messiahship was the fact that his life had fulfilled the prophecies of the Hebrew scriptures. It was this continuity that gave weight to the tradition. Thus, partly in response to Marcion, the Orthodox Church concluded that it had to decide which books would be normative for all time. This was not an easy process, for it must be remembered that, by this time, there were numerous Christian documents, all of which claimed to be legitimate.

Only after a debate that lasted until 387 C.E. did the Orthodox canon finally come to be fixed. It consisted not only of the "Old" Testament (the Hebrew Bible), but also 27 other books and letters that formed a "New" Testament. The New Testament contained the synoptic Gospels (Mark, Matthew, Luke, and John), Luke's Acts of the Apostles, as well as the letters of Paul, and selected letters of the other early missionaries.

Bet You Didn't Know

At the time of the fixing of the canon, there were numerous texts in wide circulation. In addition to the four Gospels and the Acts of the Apostles we are familiar with today, there was the Gospel of Thomas, the Gospel of Truth, the second Gospel of Matthew, the Acts of Peter, the Acts of John, and so on. Most of these texts were explicitly Gnostic in inspiration and instantly rejected; however, the case of other texts was not always so clear.

At first, the heavy Neoplatonic emphasis in the Gospel of John rendered this book suspect, but, in the end, the book was accepted by the Orthodox, as was the Revelation of John, a book of prophecies concerning Jesus' Second Coming.

Within decades of Jesus' death, Christianity had become a truly international religious tradition, and, as we have seen, the plurality of Christianities reflected the cultural diversity of the Roman Empire in Late Antiquity.

The combination of the various beliefs and practices of the times, both at the elite and popular level, was widespread and a natural part of the developing Christian tradition. On the other hand, we have also seen that in the face of such diversity, there emerged a powerful desire to unify and homogenize the tradition. The fixed canon, the co-option of monasticism, and the restricted roles of women, were but a few of the means used to create a single orthodox tradition. In the next chapter, we will discuss the development of an even more powerful tool for defending the boundaries of Orthodoxy against competing varieties of Christianity. This was the religio-political concept of Christendom.

The Least You Need to Know

- The first reason that Christianity had to be considered the fulfillment of Judaism was because if Judaism were rejected completely, Christians would have been forced to reject the validity of the Jewish scriptures, and thus the proof of Jesus' messiahship.

- The second reason that Christianity had to be considered the fulfillment of Judaism was because Christianity needed the legal protection afforded by being recognized as an "ancient tradition" to the Romans.

- The Eucharist was, and for many Christians still remains, the central symbol of Christianity, because it recreates the last meal partaken by Jesus and his disciples before his crucifixion.

- Christianity saw the recognition of the eternal gulf between people and God, between material and spiritual, as essential for maintaining the covenant with God; indeed, only by recognizing God's transcendence through action in the material world is salvation even possible.

- Neoplatonic Christianity collapsed the distance between God and people, making God immanent in the human soul and seeing the material world as a dangerous impediment.

- Only after a debate that lasted until 387 C.E. did the Orthodox canon finally become fixed, consisting not only of the "Old" Testament (the Hebrew Bible), but also 27 other books and letters that formed a "New" Testament.

Christianity from Late Antiquity to the Middle Ages

In This Chapter

- Roman Pope and Eastern Bishops
- Constantine and Christendom
- Hitting the Middle Ages
- Schism between East and West

As we shall see in this chapter and the next, the ideology of Christendom proved incredibly tenacious. However, as we shall also see, despite all efforts to the contrary, the natural tendency of the tradition was to diversify, not to unify.

The Papacy and the Patriarchates

The earliest Christian missionaries targeted largely urban populations for conversion, and this greatly influenced the subsequent "Romanization" of the Church. Indeed, missionaries such as Paul specifically targeted the regional capitals of Roman provinces. Once congregations had been established there, the bishop of the provincial capital would send out deacons to the surrounding villages to organize local congregations.

The rural congregations would then come to elect their own presbyters (priests), although these elections were always subject to the ratification of the bishop. In this way, the bishop not only came to control his own congregation, but became the focal point of all the congregations in the villages surrounding the provincial capital. A de facto agreement soon arose among the bishops that they would respect the Roman civil boundaries as the boundaries of their control.

 Divine Inspiration

The Greek word for neighborhood, that is, the area that surrounded a village, was *paroikia;* it was from this word that the English word "parish" was derived.

Because of the size of their population and their political and economic importance, certain major cities in the Roman Empire were recognized as the principal cities of their regions:

- Antioch
- Ephesus
- Alexandria
- Rome

Bishops in these cities began to assert influence over other bishops in their area, offering advice and adjudicating disputes among them.

On the Right Path

Bishops in the East came to be called patriarchs, after the biblical patriarchs. In Rome, however, this "super-bishop" came to be known as the pope, derived from the Latin word *pater* (meaning "father").

The popes in Rome were especially energetic in extending their authority over other bishops. Rome's congregation had been founded in the early first century, shortly after the founding of the Church of Jerusalem. For years, it had enjoyed a succession of skillful bishops who not only steadily increased the size of the congregation, but also managed to induce many members of the Roman upper classes to join and liberally donate money and property to the Church.

The diocese of Rome also maintained a vigorous missionary campaign throughout central Italy, and by the second century, it had dozens, if not hundreds, of congregations annexed to it. Perhaps inevitably, due to their strong position in Rome, the bishops of that city began to claim jurisdiction over disputes between bishops, not only in their immediate area, but also throughout the Empire. Moreover, the diocese in Rome had also begun an ambitious program of financial aid to congregations throughout the Empire. Considering the extreme wealth of some members of the Rome congregation, the bishops of Rome could afford to do this for an extended period of time.

Eventually, the bishops of Rome came to claim that their special destiny was to unify all the separate congregations into one unified or *catholic* (Latin word meaning "universal") church. Needless to say, the Eastern patriarchs were loath to accept this usurpation of their authority, and continued to govern their flocks with a high degree of independence. Friction mounted between the papacy (pope's reign) of Rome and the patriarchates (bishops) of the East.

Constantine and Christian Unification (Christendom)

We can only speculate about how the power struggle between the pope in Rome and the patriarchs of the East would have played out, for, before issues came to a head, another event occurred that considerably altered the development of Christianity.

The Conversion of Constantine

In the year 312, a Roman general named Constantine (306–337) was battling rivals for control of the Roman Empire. Constantine engaged and defeated the army of one of his enemies, Maxentius, outside Rome. According to legend, the night before the battle, Constantine's mother, Helena (who was a Christian), had a dream that an angel foretold victory if Constantine had the Greek monogram of

Christ on his soldiers' shields. Constantine followed this advice and won the battle and then the Empire.

Again, this is only a legend. Constantine never seems to have been baptized himself. Nevertheless, we do know that upon consolidating his power, Constantine did sign the Edict of Milan in 313, officially putting an end to the persecution of Christians in the Empire. And, in 324, when Constantine became sole emperor, he made Christianity a legally recognized religion in the Empire.

Bet You Didn't Know

Constantine also began to take an active interest in promoting Christianity. He donated large sums of money to build magnificent churches both in Rome and, later, in his new capital in Asia Minor, Constantinople. Constantine also worked to restore Jerusalem from oblivion, building the original Church of the Holy Sepulchre.

Constantine sought to take a more active role in the governance of the Church. Indeed, his professed goal was to unify all the congregations of the Empire into one centrally administered organization. However, one of the problems impeding such an ambitious plan was the fact that no one uniform set of Christian doctrines had been accepted by all the Christian congregations.

The Idea of Christendom

When a major theological controversy broke out in 324, the emperor seized the opportunity to call all the bishops of the empire together to an Ecumenical Council designed to hammer out a creed (uniform doctrinal statement) that would be binding to all Christians.

Divine Inspiration

The first Ecumenical Council was held in Nicea, Asia Minor. *Ecumenical* is the Greek word for "universal," and was applied to the council, since it was supposed to be attended by all the bishops of the Empire. In the end, however, primarily bishops from the East attended the council, although the results would have Empire-wide consequences.

The specific theological dispute addressed by the council concerned the divinity of Jesus. From his first identification as the messiah, Jesus' divine nature had not been in doubt by the majority of Christians. The exact nature of his divinity, however, had never been decided. In the years before 325, a priest named Arius (c. 250–336) from Alexandria began to teach that Jesus was not an eternal being, but that at some point God had created him. This position made Jesus divine, but something less than God. Arius' bishop, Alexander

(d. 328), disagreed: Jesus was God, and had existed forever. Arius had tremendous support among the rank and file of the churches, and the controversy threatened to split the Church.

This was the major theological controversy to which Constantine stepped in and called for the council at Nicea. There, Constantine played host to a furious debate between proponents of the Arian and Alexandrian positions, but, in the end, the party of Alexander won. The relationship between Jesus and God was defined as homoousios, meaning that Jesus and God were coequal beings "of one substance." Indeed, the council actually extended this position to include the equivalence of the *Holy Spirit* as well, creating a three-part Godhead, sometimes referred to in the West as the *Trinity*. The concrete result of the Nicene council was the formulation of a creed that enshrined this Trinitarian doctrine and specifically excluded Arianism.

Spread the Word

The **Trinity** is the Christian doctrine that defines divinity as an identity between God, Jesus, and the Holy Spirit. The **Holy Spirit,** the third person of the Trinity, is often thought of as God's guiding presence in the churches.

Ultimately, it would take three more councils for the Nicene creed to achieve its final form, but Constantine was pleased with the results, and the unification of the Church seemed a practical possibility. Just as important, the emperor had become recognized as the pivot around which the Christian Church now revolved: Church and state had, in the minds of many, become one unified whole.

Both of these perceptions were, of course, inaccurate. Christianity would have to wait until 384 for an emperor to establish the Christian religion as the official religion of the state of Rome. Moreover, Constantine's immediate successor, his son Constantius, was an Arian, and Constantius' successor even attempted to revive paganism, so the empire was soon thrown into religious chaos.

Nevertheless, the idea of Christendom—a unified Christian state—had been planted, and even the spectacular disintegration of the Roman Empire in the fourth and fifth centuries could not destroy it.

Two Distinct Branches on the Christian Tree

The defeat of Rome by the armies of the northern tribes in 410 effectively deprived the emperor in Constantinople of control over the Western half of his empire. Decades before this event, however, the Western and Eastern halves of the Empire had been drifting apart.

Geography made it difficult for the Empire to be governed from a central capital, and the fact that the Latin-speaking West and the Greek-speaking East were culturally distinct only exacerbated this problem. Christianity was not immune from the centrifugal tendencies of this division. The patriarchs of Constantinople, Alexandria, Antioch, and Jerusalem jealously guarded their independence, and had never really accepted the dominance of Rome. Moreover, despite the fact that the Ecumenical Councils had been forced to recognize Rome as the primary church, the very fact that from 325 on, the Roman emperors had resided in Constantinople, made its subordination to Rome a fiction.

Bet You Didn't Know

Many Christians in the West were uncomfortable with the idea that Jesus was of one substance with God (homoousios), and so they inserted an "iota" (letter "i") into the word to create "of similar substance" (homoiousios). As trivial as this may seem, it became one of the defining issues between the bishops of Rome and the bishops of the East.

With the fall of Rome, religious differences came to a head, and the bishops of the East universally recognized the primacy of the patriarch of Constantinople. It is from this point on that we can speak of two distinct branches of Christianity: Roman Catholicism centered on the pope in Rome and Eastern Orthodoxy centered on the patriarch of Constantinople (today, Istanbul).

In the Eastern empire, now called the Byzantine Empire, the office of Emperor would survive until the fifteenth century. Throughout the centuries, the Emperors would continue to be the de facto head of the Orthodox Church, often convening councils and interfering in religious affairs. In a sense, the dream of Constantine was fulfilled in that the Byzantine Church truly became coextensive with the state. This however did not stop division within the Orthodox world.

During the fifth and sixth centuries, for both political and theological reasons, the Ethiopian, Armenian, Syrian, and Nestorian churches had broken away from Constantinople, as had the Coptic Christians of Egypt. Such schisms were compounded by the rise of Islam in the late seventh century. Within 100 years, Muslim armies had conquered much of the old Christian heartlands, from North Africa all the way to Asia Minor. In some cases, Muslim conquest was facilitated by local Christians anxious to throw off the control of Constantinople. Amazingly, however, the Byzantine Empire would hold back the Islamic advance for almost seven centuries until the fall of Constantinople to the Muslim Turks in 1453.

The Russian Orthodox Church Hits Middle Age

Part of the Byzantine Church's losses to Islam were compensated during the Middle Ages by missionary gains made to the north on the Russian steppes and to the west in the Balkan countries. The missions to the Slavic-speaking peoples were pioneered by Cyril (826–869) and by Methodius (c. 815–885) who together reduced the Slavic language to a written script (the Cyrillic alphabet).

During the early part of the ninth century, the Bulgarians and Serbs accepted the religion of Constantinople. During the decade of 860, the Russians were converted to Orthodox Christianity and assigned a Byzantine bishop who resided at Kiev. A century later, Orthodox Christianity was made the established religion of the Russian state. In time, as the political center of gravity in Russia moved from Kiev to Moscow, so, too, did the religious center; the head of the Russian Church has resided in Moscow since 1328.

Gradually, all the Slav churches would come under Islamic domination except for the Russian Church. It was at this point that the Bishop of Moscow raised himself to the rank of patriarch in 1589. With Constantinople gone, Moscow would now be the third Rome and the center of all Christendom. Interestingly, this move almost split the Russian Church into two factions, each claiming to represent the unity of Christendom.

As with the Byzantine Emperors, the Russian Tsar (a corruption of the Latin word Caesar) sought to increase the subordination of the Russian Church to the state. The Moscow patriarch Nikon (1605–1681), on the other hand, actively sought to counteract this tendency by asserting the moral power of the Church over the state. Moreover, Nikon also hoped that the Russian Church would come to be the controlling force over the Eastern Orthodox Church at large, and, to this end, the patriarch substantially altered the Russian liturgy to bring it in line with more widespread Greek practice.

Nikon was opposed in this not only by the Tsar, but also by conservatives within his own church, who saw tampering with the Russian liturgy as an act of sacrilege. Ultimately, Nikon's liturgical alterations were kept, causing a small but vigorous group of Old Believers to break with the Church. Nikon himself, however, was deposed, and the influence of the state over the Russian Church grew with every decade. Eventually, in 1721, Tsar Peter the Great abolished the patriarchate of Moscow, and effectively made the Russian Church a department in the state bureaucracy.

The Europeans Hit Middle Age and the Papacy Loses

A similar situation, pitting king against patriarch, played itself out during the European Middle Ages, although circumstances there largely favored the popes in Rome above the kings. The fall of the Roman Empire in the West left a power vacuum that only the papacy was in a position to fill.

With the collapse of the Roman civil system, life in Europe became more local and rural in focus, with local tribal rivalries impeding the consolidation of power at a regional level. The papacy, on the other hand, maintained a clearly defined hierarchy of power radiating from Rome to the bishops in the countryside. Rome also pursued a vigorous missionary effort in the British Isles and in Northern Europe, bringing formerly pagan peoples within the orbit of Catholic Christianity. Rome, therefore, could exert influence over wide areas of Europe in ways the local civil authorities could not. What is more, the Roman Catholic Church was also one of the largest landowners in Europe.

Bet You Didn't Know

Today, the largest landowner in the world is the Roman Catholic Church. Second place belongs to McDonald's.

The high-water mark of papal power came in the thirteenth century. Throughout this period, strong political leaders emerged in France, Germany, and England, but the papacy managed to control them. Indeed, for a brief moment, during the reign of Pope Innocent III (1160–1216), Europe became unified under papal control, and by the end of the century, Pope Boniface VIII (c. 1234–1303) announced in the bull (official papal document) *Unam Sanctam* that all temporal powers everywhere must be subject to the pope.

Although a united Christendom may have seemed at hand, such unity did not last long. By the close of the thirteenth century, the gradual shift of Europe from a land-based to a cash economy had placed the papacy in increasingly difficult financial positions. At the same time, the rise of national sentiment began to have a negative effect toward central control. The latter was an especially important factor in papal decline during the fourteenth century.

When the pope attempted to interfere with the extended struggle between the English and the French, which came to be called the Hundred Years' War, the sovereigns of these two nations responded by attacking the Church and the clergy as foreign agents. Eventually, this bitter rivalry split the papacy, with two popes being elected simultaneously, one loyal to England and the other to France. Although the "Great Western Schism" (1309–1377) was eventually healed, the papacy after this incident had lost forever its position of political primacy in Europe.

Evolving Religious Practices in the Medieval West

Throughout the Middle Ages, major changes occurred in Roman Catholic doctrine and ritual. For many people during this period, baptism and the Eucharist came to represent something more than just a commemoration. They became sacraments, physical acts that, in the minds of believers, led to a direct and immediate communication with divine grace. Such an attitude, called sacramentalism in the West, assumed that certain rituals conferred grace simply by being performed. The problem with such a definition was that there was no agreement as to which rituals were sacraments and which were merely symbolic.

The Seven Sacraments

As late as the twelfth century, some 30 sacraments were still recognized by the Roman Catholic Church. Late in that century, however, the theologian Peter Lombard reduced that number to seven, which parallel the life cycle:

1. Baptism
2. Confirmation
3. Eucharist
4. Penance
5. Marriage
6. Ordination
7. *Extreme Unction*

Eventually, the seven sacraments were accepted as orthodox by Church councils and remain definitive for Roman Catholicism to this day.

 Spread the Word

Extreme Unction is a sacrament intended to facilitate physical healing or to ease death in sick or dying individuals; it is also known as Last Rites or Sacrament for the Sick.

The Importance of Penance

The development of the sacrament of penance (literally "punishment") had especially important effects on spirituality in the West. Penance is the sacrament of forgiveness for sins committed after baptism. Before the introduction of penance, post-baptismal sin was a matter for excommunication, that is, barring an individual from the Eucharist (also to be expelled from Church membership).

In time, however, mechanisms developed whereby a sinner could be reconciled to the Church through an act of repentance, typically confession of one's sins. In the West, this took on a legalistic cast, with penance being spoken of as a "compensating exchange" between the sinner and the injured party, God. Between the fourth and sixth centuries, the ritual of penance was duly formalized in the Roman Catholic Church, with weekly opportunities for confession and, then, two entire seasons set aside for public penance: Advent (the period before Christmas) and Lent (the period before Easter).

So important had the practice of penance become that by the end of the Middle Ages it was obligatory before taking the Eucharist.

Purgatory and Indulgences

It might seem that for medieval Christians, assured of forgiveness through the sacrament of penance, the afterlife would lose its terrors. This was not so. Punishment in the afterlife still remained a very real possibility since, according to Church teaching, one's penance would continue after death. *Purgatory* was the place of this post-mortem penance, and while the torments of Purgatory were not eternal, they were to be feared, nevertheless.

Medieval Christians, therefore, eagerly sought to lessen the time they would have to spend in Purgatory by participating in a variety of extra or "paraliturgical" devotions to which the pope had attached *indulgences*.

Spread the Word

Purgatory is a destination where the dead are purified of their earthly sins through suffering in preparation for admission to heaven.

Indulgences of varying degrees were granted for all manner of religious practice, for example the following:

- Endowing churches
- Saying certain prayers
- Marching in religious processions
- Undertaking hazardous journeys to distant pilgrimage shrines such as Santiago de Compostela
- Warfare (*crusade*)

Spread the Word

Indulgences assured people that by participating in extra devotions, a certain portion, usually measured in days or years, of their future stay in Purgatory would be remitted and their entrance into heaven hastened.

The greatest of the crusades, launched from the eleventh to the thirteenth centuries, were a succession of military expeditions attempting to recover Jerusalem and the Holy Land from Muslim control.

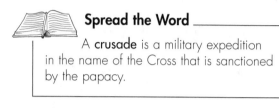

Spread the Word

A **crusade** is a military expedition in the name of the Cross that is sanctioned by the papacy.

Eastern Orthodoxy vs. Roman Catholicism

Most medieval Christians in both East and West still eagerly looked forward to the day when Christendom would again be united. However, as time went by, religious reunion between East and West was becoming increasingly unlikely. As we have seen, East and West had been pursuing divergent religious paths since the fall of Rome. As a natural result, the Eastern and Western Churches had evolved into two distinct traditions, each with its own style of being Christian. For instance, the sacraments developed differently in East and West.

Despite the proliferation of sacraments in Roman Catholicism, Orthodox theologians as late as the eighth century still spoke of only two, baptism and the Eucharist. Only in the seventeenth century did the Orthodox Church adopt the Western doctrine of the seven sacraments, and even then significant differences remained. Infants, for example, are confirmed immediately after baptism in the East, and in recognition of their full membership, children routinely receive Holy Communion from infancy on.

One of the more important sacramental differences between East and West involved the eligibility of men for ordination. Universal celibacy had been a Christian ideal since apostolic times, although this proved hardly practical as Christianity grew. Realizing this, the early Church fathers enjoined that at least the clergy should be celibate. This, too, was difficult to enforce, and there soon developed the custom of allowing presbyters (priests) to marry before ordination, although once ordained, marriage (or remarriage, in the case of the death of one's wife) was forbidden.

Bishops, however, continued to be selected from the celibate clergy, which meant in practice that most bishops came from the ranks of the monks. This two-tiered system was officially approved by the Emperor Justinian in the sixth century, and it still forms the basis of Eastern Orthodox practice to this day.

A similar system prevailed for a time in the Roman Catholic Church. However, the clergy in the West soon displayed a marked tendency to form local dynasties in which parishes were passed from father to son. Such a custom effectively undermined the central control of the papacy, and therefore the two-tiered system was gradually abandoned in the West. In the end, mandatory celibacy for all Roman Catholic clergy was legally prescribed by Pope Gregory VII in the eleventh century.

Of course, many more differences of belief and practice could be indicated between Eastern Orthodoxy and Roman Catholicism. The important point to be noted here, however, is that despite the powerful ideology of Christendom, unity could not be sustained for long, especially when there was no political power capable of imposing it.

Within a century after the death of Constantine, Christendom had fractured into two major halves, and by the Middle Ages, the two halves had hardened into two distinct styles of being Christian. This, however, was only one episode in the continuing process of Christian diversification, for, as we shall see in the next chapter, Europe now entered a period of accelerated religious change that completely shattered what was left of medieval Christendom in the West.

The Least You Need to Know

- Bishops in the East were called patriarchs after the biblical patriarchs; bishops in Rome were led by the "super-bishop" known as the pope.
- Constantine sought to unify all the congregations of the Roman Empire into one centrally administered organization, known as Christendom.
- Indulgences assured people that by participating in extra devotions, their entrance into heaven hastened.
- Within a century after the death of Constantine, Christendom had fractured into two major halves, and by the Middle Ages, the two halves had hardened into two distinct styles of being Christian (Eastern Orthodoxy and Roman Catholicism).

Reformations in the West

In This Chapter

- Franciscans and Dominicans
- Martin Luther and the Protestants
- Reformed Movement—Calvinism
- Anglicans and Presbyterians
- Catholic Reformation and the Wars of Religion

If the dream of Western Christendom united under the papacy almost became political reality in the Middle Ages, it was never at any time a religious reality. Despite the fact that some church historians have romanticized the European Middle Ages as the "Age of Faith," Europe was at no time during this period completely unified religiously. In addition to large populations of Jews and then Muslims, the papacy also had to deal with the fact that Europe played host to more than one variety of Christianity.

When the papacy began to extend its power through missions to the north during the fifth and sixth centuries, its missionaries had to contend not only with indigenous paganism, but also with Arian Christianity. Many of the Germanic peoples had been converted to Arian Christianity by missionaries from the East decades before, and it took decades more before they consented to convert to Roman Catholicism. Only in the mid-seventh century did Arian Christianity recede from Europe.

New threats to Catholic Christianity also waited in the wings. In the tenth century, a movement in Bulgaria arose that united around the teachings of a Christian priest named Bogomil. Although sporting a new mythology, Bogomil's theology was much like that taught by the Gnostic Christians of Antiquity (see Chapter 2). Rigidly dualistic, Bogomil taught that the world was created by an evil demiurge and that Jesus had been sent from God to rescue human beings from the depth of material being.

On the Right Path

Orthodox Christians believe God is separate and external from humans. Gnostics believe that knowledge of the self is the knowledge of God and that the self and the divine are the same.

Bogomil's thinking seems to have had a profound effect on a Christian movement called the Cathari ("the pure") or Albigenses, which flourished in southern France during the twelfth century. This new form of Gnosticism became so powerful and its adherents so numerous that the papacy eventually declared a holy war against it, leading to massive slaughter. Eventually, the Cathari tradition was forced underground, and disappeared from view.

Religious Reform Movements in Europe

Not all religious threats to Christian unity were imported to Western Europe: Some, like the Waldenses, were home grown. Inspired by the preaching of a layman, Peter Waldo (d. 1218), the Waldenses sought to reform the Church, and their teachings in this regard were characterized by a literal reading of the New Testament. Based on this, they claimed that only baptism and the Eucharist were legitimate sacraments, and they attempted to live lives emphasizing pacifism and poverty as Jesus did.

In time, the Waldenses had congregations throughout northern Italy, in parts of Switzerland, and in Germany. Peter Waldo had lobbied the pope for official recognition of his movement, but Waldo's preaching was seen as too radical, and his petition was denied. The Waldenses persisted despite persecution, and still survive to this day as an autonomous Christian group.

Religious reform movements were many during this period, and not all met with persecution. Indeed, some movements were accepted by the Roman Catholic Church and incorporated into its fabric. Tiring of the insular nature of the monastic lifestyle, many monks during the twelfth and thirteenth centuries abandoned their monasteries in order to do service in the larger society. Called friars (from the Latin word *frater*, meaning "brother"), these monks sought a life that balanced teaching and preaching in the world with adherence to a modified monastic rule. In time, new monastic orders coalesced around these new rules.

The Friar Clubs

Two groups of friars that arose virtually simultaneously in the thirteenth century became the Franciscan and Dominican Orders.

Based on the teachings of Francis of Assisi (1182–1226), the Franciscan Order emphasized the importance of simple preaching and public service while living a life of apostolic poverty. It was recognized by the pope in 1210. In time, the Franciscan Order would become as worldly as the rest of the Church, but in the days of the first Franciscans, the Friars Minor, as they were called, lived nomadic lives, begging for their food and avoiding the accumulation of property.

The Dominicans, on the other hand, while demanding austerity of their members, nevertheless sought a more settled and regular existence. Moreover, unlike the Franciscans, the Dominicans emphasized learning and scholarship, and were instrumental in creating schools and colleges throughout Europe. Although officially recognized by the pope only in 1216, the Order had been founded some years earlier by a Spaniard named Dominic de Guzman (1170–1221).

As a young man, Dominic had been sent to southern France in order to convert the Albigensians to Catholic Christianity, a job he pursued with relish. From the beginning, then, the detection and suppression of dissent and heterodox beliefs was one of the primary goals of the Dominicans. In time, the Dominican Order would become a guiding force of the Inquisition, a special court set up by the pope to combat heresy throughout Europe.

The Fragments and Splinters

Although heresy was perceived to be on the rise in the thirteenth century, the Christian fragmentation of Europe really began to accelerate in earnest in the fourteenth and fifteenth centuries. In the 1360s, an English cleric named John Wycliffe (1328–84) proposed a number of ideas for the reform of the Church that would become increasingly popular in the coming decades.

Across the European continent, similar demands for reform were being heard, this time in Bohemia (the modern-day Czech Republic). There, a charismatic leader named Jan Hus (1373–1415) was proposing many of the same ideas as Wycliffe from his pulpit in Prague. Despite the support of the Bohemian king, Hus was burned at the stake at the order of the pope in 1415. His death set off a virtual religious revolution in Bohemia. Dozens of splinter groups, with names such as Hussites, Horebites, and Taborites, arose, each demanding independence from Rome. Eventually the majority of the Bohemian Church reunited with Rome, while some held fast, including the *Unitas Fratrum*, also known today as the Moravians.

The Protestant Reformation

Despite the constant calls for reform of the Church of Rome, it was not until the sixteenth century that a fortuitous coincidence of political necessity and the forceful imagination of one person would combine to spark the massive explosion known as the Protestant Reformation. Martin Luther (1483–1546) was an Augustinian monk and professor of theology who taught at the University of Wittenberg in northern Germany.

A conscientious cleric, Luther avidly followed the impact of Rome's policies—especially fundraising activities—on his local parishioners. In 1517, Pope Leo X (1475–1521) was searching for ways to finance his ambitious rebuilding projects in Rome, especially the reconstruction of Constantine's old St. Peter's basilica.

One of the methods typically used for such projects was the selling of indulgences. Although a common practice, Luther believed that this was being abused by the Church. In order to stimulate debate on the issue, Luther posted on the door of the Wittenberg church a list of 95 theses questioning the pope's power to issue such indulgences. The response was remarkable. The theses were published through the medium of the newly invented printing press, and soon copies were circulated throughout Europe.

Despite the triviality of the topic, the theology behind the sale of indulgences seemed to symbolize all that was wrong about the Church, and crystallized anti-Church opposition. Luther's theses became the topic of debate between religious orders, and political leaders smelled opportunity in these divisions. Eventually, Luther was called to account by both the Church and the Holy Roman Emperor who held nominal control over Germany. Luther, however, refused to stop his questioning, and the pressure put on him forced him to take up increasingly radical positions. Indeed, Luther eventually went so far as to publicly embrace the teachings of Jan Hus (burned at the stake for heresy).

Bet You Didn't Know

Despite the widespread perception of Church corruption throughout Europe and among Germans in particular, Luther at first seemed to have had no desire to break with the Church. Nevertheless, like the Apostle Paul before him, Luther was forced by his opponents to develop a theology to support his position. In it, he adopted positions of Hus, such as the primacy of scripture, but he went further than Hus.

Earlier in his theological career, Luther had pacified doubts about his salvation by returning to the writings of Paul. Paul, of course, emphasized the importance of faith in Jesus over the old Jewish-Christian emphasis on ritual work, as prescribed in the Hebrew Bible. Luther saw a parallel between Paul's situation and his own. Like the early Jewish Christians, the Roman Catholic Church, Luther argued, had mistakenly come to teach that ritual work was at least as important as faith. Paul, however, had taught that faith alone "justified" (saved) a sinner, and that this faith was the product of God's grace—grace that God freely gave to believers as a gift, not in exchange for ritual work. This was the position Luther adopted, effectively calling into question the entire sacramental system of the Roman Catholic Church.

Such notions were considered heresy by the leaders of the Church. Luther was duly excommunicated by the pope (1519) and declared an outlaw by the Holy Roman Emperor (1521). Nevertheless, the political situation in Germany at the time was such that the divisions caused by the emerging Lutheran movement were politically advantageous to some local princes. Luther remained safe under their protection, and the movement thrived in many of the small principalities of Germany.

Eventually the emperor attempted to reimpose religious unity by force, but this was unsuccessful. The emperor was forced to issue an edict that allowed the princes of Germany to decide for themselves whether their lands were to be Catholic or Lutheran. When, in 1529, the emperor attempted to revoke the edict, the Lutheran princes "protested," which gave rise to the term Protestant. Germany then sank into a state of constant conflict until 1555, when the old edict was reconfirmed with the Peace of Augsburg. However, this, too, was merely a temporary peace. In time, the war between Catholics and Protestants would engulf all of Europe and last for nearly a century more.

The Reformed Traditions

Meanwhile, other reform-minded people were beginning to follow in Luther's footsteps. Ulrich Zwingli (1484–1531) of Switzerland, for example, had independently come to conclusions very similar to Luther's. Zwingli accepted the scriptures as the sole authority for the Church, taught salvation by faith alone, and, like Luther, rejected all but the biblically based sacraments of baptism and the Eucharist. Zwingli's reforms were accepted in Zurich and spread to other areas of Switzerland, Germany, and France. By the time of Zwingli's death in 1531, the Reformed Movement (so-called to differentiate it from more moderate Lutheranism) had built sizable momentum.

The Reformed Movement found its next great leader in a French lawyer named John Calvin (1509–1564). Calvin took a leaf from Zwingli's book and set about making another Swiss city a showcase for his reforms. Calvin's Geneva would, in time, become the international center for the Reformed tradition, sending missionaries throughout the European continent as well as to England and Scotland.

Calvin, too, was a theological innovator. He took Luther's emphasis on the transcendence of God to its logical conclusion. If, indeed, God held absolute sovereignty over his creation, Calvin reasoned that this must mean that God wills everything, including the eventual salvation or damnation of individual human beings. Moreover, absolute sovereignty logically means that God must have known from the beginning of time who would be saved and who would be damned. Such a doctrine is called predestination. After Calvin articulated this doctrine in his massive *Institutes of the Christian Religion*, it became a hallmark of the Reformed Movement, also known as Calvinism.

Divine Inspiration

The Five Points of Calvinism are easily remembered by the acronym TULIP:

Total depravity—Sin has extended to every part of humanity's personality.

Unconditional election—God alone has determined who is destined for glory and who for damnation.

Limited atonement—Christ died to atone for specific sins of specific sinners and to make the Church holy.

Irresistible grace—All who God elects will come to learn about him.

Perseverance of the saints—The saints that God has saved will remain in his hands until they are glorified and brought to be with him in heaven.

The Radical Reformation

The Lutheran and Reformed Churches still shared with the Roman Catholic Church the desire for a united Christendom—united, of course, under either the Lutheran or Reformed banner. To this end, the leaders of the Lutheran and Reformed movements still held to the idea of a territorial Church, that is, a Church that all residents of a country were obligated to attend.

To some Protestants, however, such a conception of the Church was no less tyrannous than that of the Roman Catholic Church. These Protestants argued that the Christian Church should be voluntary, with only true believers admitted to fellowship. One such group, perhaps influenced by the earlier Cathari and Waldenses, formed in Switzerland during the 1520s. As a symbol of the voluntary nature of their church, this group insisted that infant baptism was wrong, since baptism was only valid when it was undertaken by an adult who freely chose it. Infant baptism, they pointed out, appears nowhere in the Bible. Called Anabaptists ("rebaptizers") by their opponents, they were ferociously persecuted by Catholics, Lutherans, and Reformed Protestants alike, since their voluntary church was seen as a threat to the social order.

Despite this persecution, made all the worse by their pacifistic convictions, Anabaptists spread from Switzerland throughout the continent. One famous Anabaptist group was founded by Menno Simons (1496–1561) in the Netherlands. In time, the Mennonites experienced such persecution that they were forced to emigrate first to Poland, then to Russia, and eventually to the New World, where their descendants live to this day. The old-style Amish are one surviving branch of the Mennonites in America.

> **Bet You Didn't Know**
>
> Mennonites have long been known for the stance they take for peace (because Jesus taught the way of peace, openness, and acceptance of others' differences). Because of this, many Mennonites choose to not join the military or pay the portion of their income taxes that go toward military spending.

Reformation in England

The British Isles were not immune from the forces that fractured Christendom in the sixteenth century. In fact, each of the continental branches of Protestantism found counterparts across the Channel in England and Scotland. In 1534, King Henry VIII (1509–1547), acting largely from political motives, pressured Parliament into passing a series of Acts that effectively nationalized the Roman Church, creating the Church of England with Henry as its head.

The Church of England, or Anglicanism, retained much of the structure of Roman Catholicism, both in terms of Episcopal administration and in the liturgy. In time, Anglican doctrine would come to be influenced by Lutheran and Reformed ideas, but in the end it remained perhaps the most conservative movement to emerge out of the Protestant Reformation.

Scotland, on the other hand, came under the direct influence of the Reformed Tradition, specifically Calvinism. Scottish Calvinism was adamant in its replacement of the old Episcopal structure with one in which local congregations, grouped into presbyteries, maintained more independence from any centralized control. In time, Presbyterianism would come to have a major impact within England, and was, in part, responsible for the rise of a radical reform movement within Anglicanism itself during the seventeenth century.

These "Puritans," as they were called, attempted to force the larger Anglican Church into adopting more radical reforms along the lines of the continental Calvinists. While ultimately unsuccessful, elements of Puritanism nevertheless survived independent of the Anglican Church, especially in America, where the movement metamorphosed into Congregationalism. England also had its representative of the Radical Reformation. The English Baptists, for example, were influenced by the continental Anabaptists (although a strong streak of Calvinism ran through English Baptism as well).

Varieties of Protestant Worship

One of the legacies of the Reformation was the modification of medieval religious practices. Few of the churches that emerged out of the Reformation, for example, retained intact the entire Roman Catholic liturgical calendar. Some, such as the Lutheran and Anglican Churches, kept most of the yearly structure intact, although saints' days were de-emphasized.

The Reformed Churches of the continent and Scottish Presbyterians went a bit further, retaining only the major festivals of Christmas, Easter, and Pentecost, and, in some cases, rejecting even these. In all cases, the Reformers wished to de-emphasize the Christian year, which, in their eyes, had largely become an excuse for disorderly and impious celebration.

In contrast, the Reformation traditions sought to re-emphasize the sanctity of the Sabbath. To this end, the Reformers tended to change Sunday services in a variety of ways, although much of the basic structure of the old Catholic Mass was retained. An important change, however, was that all Protestant churches came to conduct Sunday services in the local language, and not in Latin, so that the laity actually understood what was being said. In addition, unlike the Catholic Mass, a certain amount of lay participation was also encouraged. Congregational singing became popular, and often local folk tunes were pressed into service for use in hymns.

It was among the Radical Reformers that the most sweeping liturgical changes appeared. Anabaptists simplified Sunday services even further than did the Lutheran and Reformed churches. Extemporaneous preaching and spontaneous prayer by the laity were encouraged, and the Eucharist de-emphasized even more. In some cases, as among the Baptists, the availability of the Eucharist came to be limited to four times a year. In a very few instances, the Radical Reformers went so far as to do away with the old Sabbath practices altogether.

The English Quakers, for example, rejected all outward rituals, since they believed that the indwelling spirit was a permanent connection to God. To this day, therefore, some Quaker meetings have no leader and no set pattern. At such Quaker services, members will sit quietly at their pews until one of their number is moved to speak by the Holy Spirit. If one is so moved to speak, this is the day's sermon. Occasionally no one speaks, and Sunday meetings end with no action at all, apart from silent prayer. The simplicity of this kind of service is indeed a long way from the complexity and grandeur of the Roman Catholic Mass.

The Catholic Reformation

As Christendom began to fragment under the impact of the Protestant Reformation, the leaders of the Catholic Church were not idle, but entered into a period of profound soul-searching and vigorous internal reform. The resulting Catholic Reformation (sometimes known as the "Counter-Reformation") did little to stem the religious diversification of Europe, but it did spiritually reinvigorate the Roman Catholic Church.

The Catholic Reformation was pursued at many levels and in many ways. For example, as it became increasingly clear that the Protestant revolt was no temporary aberration, the Church called a general council in order to propose its own reform program and to chart a strategy for bringing Europe back to the Roman fold.

Benefits of the Council of Trent

Meeting from 1545 to 1563, the Council of Trent's stated goal was to address the "evils that have long afflicted and well-nigh overwhelmed the Christian commonwealth." Such evils were seen as both doctrinal and institutional. During the Council's lengthy sessions, the orthodox Catholic position concerning such things as original sin and justification, the role of scripture, the relationship of works to faith, and the nature and number of the sacraments, were debated and clarified.

The Council also sought to rectify abuses by the clergy, abuses both institutional (for example, multiple office-holding, the buying of clerical offices, neglect of the laity) and personal (for example, immoral living, illiteracy, or general ignorance of Church doctrine).

While in the end the Council of Trent largely reaffirmed traditional positions, it nevertheless clarified dogma, improved the efficiency of the Church's organization, raised standards for the clergy, and generally re-emphasized the necessity of spiritual discipline at all levels to face the Protestant challenge.

The Piety (or Psychology) of St. Theresa and St. John

It was perhaps at the level of basic Christian spirituality, however, that the Catholic Reformation had its greatest impact, for, in addition to the institutional changes, it also fostered an intense Christian piety that came to permeate all levels of Catholic society. This piety is perhaps best illustrated by the writings of the great Spanish mystics, St. Teresa of Avila (1515–1582) and St. John of the Cross (1542–1591). Both were active in the reform of Spanish monasticism, but they are better remembered today for such spiritual classics as St. Teresa's *The Interior Castle* (c. 1577) and St. John's *The Dark Night of the Soul* (c. 1578).

In *The Interior Castle*, St. Teresa presents the reader with a kind of mystical manual, systematically setting out the stages of mystical ascent by using the image of the soul as a crystalline castle with seven concentric rooms. In simple but powerful language, Teresa then documents the effects of prayer, asceticism, and spiritual purity, as the soul progresses deeper into this castle, in the center of which lies an overwhelming experience of divinity itself. Indeed, *The Interior Castle* culminates with one of the most vivid and thrilling descriptions of an encounter with God to be found in all of mystical literature.

St. John, on the other hand, saw the mystical quest for God in much darker terms, poetically likening it to the anguish felt by a lover searching for his beloved. Such anguish was necessary in order to lead the soul beyond self-love, thus readying it for the "dark night of the soul," a state in which God spiritually purifies the soul and makes it fit for the beatific vision.

Despite their differences, however, both St. Teresa and St. John had a profound intuitive knowledge of human psychology, and both were masters at communicating to their readers a passionate and compelling vision of the mystical quest. In time, these books would become mystical touchstones not only for Catholics, but for mystics everywhere.

The Wars of Religion and the End of Christendom

Although it must seem to the observer today that Christendom in Europe was irreversibly shattered by the end of the sixteenth century, many of the great Catholic powers, such as Spain and France, acted as though it could still be reconstituted under their leadership. The King of Spain, for example, attempted to reimpose Catholicism in the Netherlands, but he was only partially successful due to the opposition of England.

Bet You Didn't Know

Both St. Teresa of Avila's *The Interior Castle* and St. John of the Cross's *The Dark Night of the Soul* are still in print today, and can be found at your local library or online book retailer.

A series of French kings attempted to wipe out followers of the Reformed Tradition, called Huguenots, in their territories. This, too, was only partially successful. Such conflicts, however, only heightened tensions between Protestants and Catholics, and shortly after the beginning of the seventeenth century, Europe was on the brink of an all-out religious conflict that would last some three decades.

The Wars of Religion eventually engulfed nearly all the European states, spreading death and creating economic chaos everywhere. Little was gained, and the conflict degenerated into a protracted war of attrition. Exhaustion finally brought the participants to the negotiating table in 1648. The Treaty of Westphalia, which ended the Wars of Religion, did little more than ratify the religious situation that had been in place with the Peace of Augsburg almost a century before. Much had changed, however.

Bet You Didn't Know

Searching for religious freedom, more than 200,000 French Huguenots fled to countries such as England, Germany, South Africa, Switzerland, and America. More than 5,000 Huguenots reached America's shores between 1618 and 1725.

Little confidence remained in the ideology of Christendom, which had survived so tenaciously since the days of Constantine. As we have seen, the idea of Christendom never completely died, although, as Europe now entered the modern age, many Europeans were weary of all things religious.

The Least You Need to Know

- The Roman Catholic Church incorporated some of the many reform movements during the Reformation, such as the Franciscan and Dominican Orders of friars.

- Because Martin Luther believed that some of the common practices of the Roman Catholic Church, such as the selling of indulgences, were being abused, he eventually formed the Lutheran Church, and the term "Protestants" arose.

- The Church of England, or Anglicanism, retained much of the structure of Roman Catholicism.

- During the Catholic Reformation, the Council of Trent largely reaffirmed traditional positions, clarified dogma, improved the efficiency of the Church's organization, raised standards for the clergy, and generally re-emphasized the necessity of spiritual discipline at all levels, to face the Protestant challenge.

- The Wars of Religion spread death and economic chaos to nearly all the European states, until the participants came to the negotiating table in 1648 for the Treaty of Westphalia.

The Clash Between Modernity and Christianity

In This Chapter

- Education in the modern city
- Age of Reason and Enlightenment
- America's Christian diversity
- The Pious, Methodic, and Awakened Ones
- Sectarian Mormons and Adventists

With the influx of people to large cities and new lands, religion, as usual, became a hotbed of debate as new forms of Christianity developed and splintered. This chapter will explore some of these new forms, and chart the larger history of the still-unresolved clash between modernity and Christianity that continues to this day.

Europe on the Up and Up

As the fortunes of the papacy rose and fell, Europe itself was undergoing a startling transformation. Regional economies were growing, trade was expanding, and cities were once again becoming a common feature of the European landscape. An urban culture developed in which the arts and sciences quickly began to flourish. During this time, not only did great Gothic cathedrals begin to appear, but also a new kind of institution of higher learning, the university.

The Rise of Cathedrals

A cathedral is simply a bishop's church, and, as such, it is named for a symbol of his office, the *cathedra* or bishop's chair. Cathedrals, therefore, had existed since Christian Roman times. Beginning in the twelfth century, however, innovative engineering techniques were combined with a new architectural vocabulary to create an entirely new building style for cathedrals.

Originating in Northern Europe, homeland of the Goths of Antiquity, this new building style came to be known as "Gothic." Compared with its predecessor, the Gothic cathedral was taller, larger, and more highly decorated. Pointed arches replaced rounded arches, and walls were designed to accommodate huge banks of stained glass windows, flooding the new building with brilliantly colored light.

The great cathedrals were many things to many people. To the average European, they must have seemed a gateway into another world. Most likely visiting from the countryside, such a person would have been struck by the sheer immensity of the building, its vertical space perhaps evoking emotions of awe and wonder. The stonework itself, climbing high into the sky with improbably little support, must have seemed the very definition of a miracle.

Bet You Didn't Know

Cities such as Paris, Chartres, and Amiens began to compete to see which could build the tallest and most grandiose Gothic cathedral. Taking an army of skilled craftsmen years if not decades to build, the Gothic cathedrals were, therefore, not only expressions of Christian piety, but also expressions of rising civic pride.

Along with the emotional reaction, however, the Gothic cathedral also provided the average European with intellectual stimulation. Almost every surface of the cathedral was decorated, both inside and out. Everywhere a person turned, he or she would see a painted mural, a mosaic, a sculpture, or a colored window depicting either biblical scenes, biblical symbols, or, in some cases, even visual representations of Church doctrines. Indeed, most Gothic cathedrals were explicitly designed to be the "Bibles of the poor."

The builders of the cathedrals were careful to draw on those Christian motifs and symbols that were instantly recognizable to anyone, regardless of social class or education. Thus, while poor and illiterate, the average European of the day could "read" the Gothic cathedral nevertheless, and people probably took away from their visits to the cathedral not only a greater devotion to the Christian faith, but also a greater understanding of that faith.

If the great cathedrals of Europe were important for the development of popular religion, they were equally important for the development of some of the West's more elite forms of Christianity. It is from the great cathedrals of Europe, for example, that the early universities sprang.

Higher Learning

With the rise of the cities, however, cathedral schools became popular alternatives to the rural monasteries because they were more readily accessible to the urban elite. Like the monastery schools, the cathedral schools offered a curriculum featuring the seven liberal arts of classical Antiquity: grammar, logic, rhetoric, arithmetic, geometry, astronomy, and music. In those cities with multiple cathedral schools, the professors and students would often band together to safeguard their rights and privileges. The resulting "learning" guild was called a *universitas* (now known as a university).

The universities inspired Europe to greater levels of intellectual vigor and sophistication, and out of these institutions of higher learning there arose a plethora of philosophical and theological systems. By far, the most influential of these systems was scholasticism. Scholastic theologians were primarily interested in reconciling reason with faith, and in discerning the limits of both.

> ### On the Right Path
>
> In most cities, the universitas remained closely associated with the cathedral schools, but in larger European cities such as Paris and Bologna, the universitas came to be chartered by the local authorities as a separate institution, endowed with its own facilities and buildings. Such independent universities continued to offer the traditional seven liberal arts, but soon expanded their curriculum to include graduate studies in law, medicine, and theology. These were the forerunners of the modern Western university.

Since the twelfth century, questions about the relationship between reason and faith had become ever more pressing, for it was during that time that the works of the ancient Greek philosopher, Aristotle (384–322 B.C.E.), first became generally available in Europe. Unlike Plato his teacher, Aristotle taught that knowledge of spiritual things could reliably be obtained through the use of reason. Revelation was relatively unimportant therefore, because, according to Aristotle, the human intellect could inductively reason from the material world to the reality of God. So prestigious was Aristotle's reputation that his rationalism could not be easily ignored. Thus, great scholastic theologians such as Anselm of Canterbury (1033–1109) and Peter Lombard (c. 1100–1160) would spend their lives wrestling mightily with the implications of Aristotle's philosophy.

Of all the scholastics of that era, it was Thomas Aquinas (1224–1274) who created the most balanced—and influential—synthesis of faith and reason. In works such as the *Summa Contra Gentiles* and the *Summa Theologica* (a work that some have compared to a great Gothic cathedral in its immensity and complexity), Aquinas sought to show that, while revelation was indeed above human reason, reason nevertheless could complement revelation by proving its probable truth. In so doing, reason could deepen one's understanding of the saving doctrines of the faith, although reason alone could never achieve these doctrines as Aristotle had taught. Although the powerful "Thomist" synthesis would eventually be proclaimed the official theology of the Roman Catholic Church in the nineteenth century, it did little to settle the scholastic debates of the day.

Some theologians, such as Duns Scotus (c. 1265–1308) and William of Ockham (c. 1285–1347), attacked the Thomist synthesis, arguing that it gave too high a precedence to human reason. Predictably, others attacked it from the opposite perspective, and, at times, scholastic theologians of all camps went to absurd lengths to prove their points. Nevertheless, despite their excesses, the scholastic debates of this era did anticipate many of the debates over reason and revelation that would continue on through modernity to trouble Western Christianity to the present day.

Modernity

Beginning in the seventeenth century, Europe entered a period of massive and prolonged change—change that would revolutionize the West and have far-reaching consequences for the rest of the world. This era, now called by historians the modern period, was marked by the successive rise of rationalism, science, political liberalism and secularism, industrialization, and imperialism. The origins of these new ideologies and institutions were complex and in some cases obscure, but their overall impact can be summed up in a single word: modernity.

Modernity represented a peculiarly new worldview in human history. In its approach to the world, modernity emphasized skepticism and critical thinking, as well as a positive attitude toward social and intellectual change. Modernity also tended to de-emphasize the importance of divine revelation as a source of knowledge, and insisted on the paramount role of the individual in shaping the future.

Although modernity dominated the period, it is clear that at no time did it actually triumph over and completely replace the premodern Christian worldviews—even in the West. Christianity actually experienced unprecedented growth and global expansion during this period. Moreover, the struggle of the Christian churches to respond and, in some cases, to adapt to modernity led to many new and novel forms of the tradition.

Religion and the Enlightenment

The Reformation effectively broke the hold of a millennium and a half of Roman Catholic tradition dictating Christian orthodoxy in Europe. Indeed, without the support of tradition, the inherent ambiguity of biblical revelation became obvious to all—a fact amply demonstrated by the fragmented development of the Reformation. Moreover, the subsequent Wars of Religion revealed the futility of reimposing a single orthodoxy by force.

For those in power in Europe, therefore, little could be done except to tolerate the de facto diversity of Christianities and get on with the business of governing. Such an attitude fostered a much more pragmatic approach to ordering human relations. The manifest success of this approach—nearly a century and a half of relative peace in Europe after 1648—further eroded the centrality of revelation in political policy.

 Bet You Didn't Know

Some modern ideologies, such as the communism based on the thought of Karl Marx (1818–1883), was militantly antireligious and rigorously materialistic. As such, modernity confronted Christianity with a worldview entirely at odds with the old premodern worldviews inherited from Antiquity.

Ultimately, political liberals came to see the state as a product of human endeavor, not the will of God, and therefore the desire for religious unity came to be seen as less relevant in the political processes of

Europe. This encouraged an environment of relative toleration for religious dissidents. In time, England, Prussia, and Austria moved toward official policies of religious toleration, whereas in France, toleration became an unspoken understanding.

Applying Human Reason

In addition to religious toleration, the events of the sixteenth and seventeenth centuries also accelerated another, more fundamental intellectual controversy developing for centuries: What are the limits of human reason in the production of knowledge?

With the Reformation and the subsequent Wars of Religion, the status of revelation began to wane. European philosophers and theologians began to probe the limits of reason again, and this time, freed to a certain degree from the dictates of religious institutions, they drew more radical conclusions than their medieval counterparts.

The French philosopher René Descartes (1596–1650), for example, developed a system that doubted everything but the reality of the thinker's own mind. All facts, according to Descartes, could only find their origin within the human mind, and therefore all reliable knowledge could only be that which is synthesized by human reason.

On the other hand, the English philosopher John Locke (1632–1704) started from very different premises. According to Locke, all facts came through the five senses and the empirical observation of nature. Nevertheless, the end result was the same for Locke as it was for Descartes: The knowledge produced by these facts was ultimately the product of human reason. This renewed emphasis on reason and on the ability of human beings to make valid judgments based on knowledge was seen by many to finally mark the end of the so-called "Dark Ages" of the medieval centuries and the beginning of a new "Age of Enlightenment."

> ### On the Right Path
> It was René Descartes who said, "I think, therefore I am."

Enter the Age of Enlightenment

Despite the emphasis on rationalism, the Enlightenment was not an anti-religious or anti-Christian age. Indeed, Descartes intended his new philosophical system to be a new and better way for individuals to know God. John Locke wrote books with such titles as *The Reasonableness of Christianity* (1695) to prove rationally the divinity of Jesus and the historicity of his miracles.

The Enlightenment could, however, be anti-clerical and anti-institutional. Enlightenment thinkers tended to paint the Roman Catholic Church as the epitome of medieval irrationalism and supernaturalism, and the philosopher Voltaire's (1694–1778) motto, *"Ecrasez l'infame!"* (Crush the infamous thing!), is a good indication of the vehemence of such attitudes toward the Church in France. Nevertheless, even Voltaire recognized the importance of religion in human life, especially in terms of ethical behavior and the cohesion of society. For, while it was believed that a "natural" ethical code could be derived rationally, it was still firmly believed by many Enlightenment thinkers that only divine origin could account for the peculiar force of humanity's ethical conscience in the first place.

On the other hand, as long as Christians of all sects recognized their common ethical core, there was no justification for violent disputes over the meaning of revelation, nor was there any reason for imposing interpretive unity. Ethical unity, they argued, allowed for religious diversity. In the end, religion was simply a matter of personal choice, to be made according to the dictates of one's own conscience. For reasons largely of pragmatic necessity, this was an ideology that would find its earliest and most successful expression in the English Americas.

Christian Diversity in English America

From the beginning of English settlement in the seventeenth century, the American colonies attracted a wide variety of Christian traditions, from Anglicans and Catholics, to Lutherans and Reformed, as well as the various kinds of Radical Reformation sects. Thus, while the Church of England remained the formally established church in many of the colonies, this had little meaning since no one church could claim a clear majority.

Toleration of other brands of Protestantism (and, in time, Catholicism and Judaism) became a social necessity, especially in the Middle Colonies. New York, for example, had originally been a colony of the Dutch. For expediency's sake, when the English annexed the colony in 1664, the Dutch Reformed Church was officially recognized and its rights preserved. Indeed, the Duke of York opted for a policy of outright religious toleration, and the colony soon attracted French Calvinists, German Lutherans, New England Congregationalists, Quakers, Baptists, Mennonites, Catholics, and Jews. With the founding of Pennsylvania in 1681, William Penn followed a similar course, with the added novelty of extending religious toleration to Native Americans (an experiment of sadly short duration).

By the time the English colonies eventually achieved their independence in 1781, religious tolerance had become the norm, although making it the official policy of the new federal government was still hotly debated. New Englanders, for example, argued that such a policy would undermine the established status of the Congregational Church in their region. Others argued that such toleration would lead to America's becoming a sink for dissenters, antinomians (those who believed they were bound by no ethical laws), and non-Christians.

However, many of the Founding Fathers, such as Thomas Jefferson, were in favor of incorporating tolerance into the national framework. Also, various churches of the Radical Reformation, victims as they were of oppression in Europe, demanded complete freedom from territorial churches in the United States. Baptists were especially vocal during the Constitutional Convention about the issue of religious freedom. Eventually, the First Amendment of the American Constitution (1791) explicitly stated that the federal government should be completely neutral in regards to religion and, unlike Europe, no church would enjoy establishment status. This led to what has come to be called *denominationalism*, the idea that all religious groups in the United States were equal in the eyes of the law.

Spread the Word

Denominationalism is the separation of Christian tradition into a number of autonomous voluntary organizations.

Protestant Pietism and Religious Revivalism

The Age of Enlightenment was a period of contrasts and contradictions. Although important for the rise of rationalism, the period was important as well for the contrary movements it engendered, especially in the religious sphere. If, on the one hand, the Enlightenment encouraged the search for a more rational Christianity, it also proved a catalyst for new Christian movements that sought to place the non-rational and experiential elements of the tradition above overly rationalized doctrinal elements. Such a movement was *Pietism*.

Pious Pietism

Pietism actually finds its roots in the period prior to the Enlightenment, in the early seventeenth century. During this period, many continental Protestants, while appalled by the Wars of Religion, were also alarmed by the flagging religious enthusiasm that was evident by the wars' end. They found their pastors lackluster and dry, and they feared that Protestantism was slipping into a kind of inflexible scholasticism (see the previous section on "Higher Learning").

Spread the Word

Pietism was a Protestant movement that sought to place the nonrational and experiential elements of the tradition above overly rationalized doctrinal elements.

In response, some Protestants began to stress a more personal faith based on the idea of true piety. Piety, as defined by one of the leaders of the movement, Philipp Jacob Spener (1635–1705), meant right feeling as well as right believing. Right feeling, in turn, meant the cultivation of an intense personal experience of God, as well as an intense desire to bring this Gospel message to others. Pietism seems to have originated among the Dutch Reformed Churches, but by the end of the eighteenth century it had spread to Lutheranism in both Germany and Scandinavia, and had become a hallmark of a revived Moravian Church.

The following century—the so-called "Age of
Reason"—Pietism came into its own and experienced
its greatest growth. Indeed, we find in the eighteenth
century the rise of perhaps the most famous of Pietist
sects, the Methodists of John Wesley (1703–1791).
As a young man, Wesley, who grew up in England
within the Anglican Church, began to search for a
more meaningful religious experience. To this end,
he and his brother Charles formed a college club to
pursue disciplined Bible study.

The methodical nature of the club inspired the nick-
name, Methodists. In 1738, Wesley came into contact with the Moravians on a journey to America.
Impressed by their simple piety, and subsequently
undergoing a powerful mystical experience of his
own, Wesley made the cultivation of true piety the
goal of Methodism.

The First Great Awakening

Perhaps an even better indicator of the power of
Protestant Pietism during the eighteenth century was
the fact that the century witnessed two massive waves
of religious *revivalism* in Europe and America, both
of which were strongly pietistic in character. The
first wave, called the "Great Awakening," began
roughly around 1720 and peaked in 1740. The origins of the Great Awakening are obscure, but it has
been suggested that the combination of the Pietist
message, with a renewed interest in *millennialism*,
sparked the revival.

Millennialism is the ancient Christian idea that
Christ's Second Coming was imminent. Combined

with Pietism, millennialism created a great urgency to convert as many people as possible before the end. The means did not necessarily matter, nor necessarily did the denomination. Thus, we find during this period ministers of almost all Protestant persuasions preaching wherever they could find a crowd—whether in a church or an open field, it did not matter. In time, this democratic style of preaching, as well as its content of millennial Pietism, came to form a pan-denominational movement, which later generations would call *Evangelical Protestantism*.

 Spread the Word

Revivalism is the large-scale movements of religious enthusiasm, sometimes lasting for months or years. **Millennialism** is the Christian belief that the Last Judgment will be preceded by Jesus' Second Coming to Earth and his establishment of a thousand years of peace and prosperity—the millennium.

Well after 1740, Evangelical Protestantism continued to thrive in Europe, especially in England, although the fire of revival cooled somewhat. In America, however, both Evangelical Protestantism *and* revivalism became permanent features of the American religious landscape. Indeed, it is difficult to date the conclusion of the Great Awakening in America since it seems not to have ended, but rather to have evolved into a successive series of local revivals that continued throughout the century. Moreover, by the end of the century, the country found itself in the grip of yet another national religious revival—the Second Great Awakening.

 Spread the Word

> **Evangelical Protestantism** is a broad movement that developed within Protestantism in the eighteenth century that emphasizes a democratic style of preaching, millennialism, and Pietism.

The Second Great Awakening

Lasting roughly from 1790 to 1840, the Second Great Awakening was especially powerful on the United States' rapidly expanding western frontier. Here, the largely unchurched frontier population would flock to "camp meetings" to hear a succession of fiery, if unlettered, evangelical preachers. Such camp meetings, outdoor revivals that lasted several days or weeks, provided one of the single-most important sources of religious experience for the inhabitants of the American frontier.

At the center of the camp, the organizers of the meeting would build a raised preaching platform, with benches stretching out in front. Here campers would sit for hours, listening in captivated attention to preachers of several denominations detailing the awful wages of sin and urging every heart to repent. In the evening, the preaching marathon would often reach an emotional climax. People would spontaneously break out into shouts or shrieks, begin to cry or dance, or be overcome with uncontrollable bodily spasms.

Bet You Didn't Know

Camp meetings eventually took on a fairly established structure, even though they originally seemed to be chaotic. Typically, a centrally located rural place was designated well in advance, and dozens of families from the surrounding countryside would congregate there at the appointed time. Upon arrival, each family would pitch a large tent and set up their cooking pots in preparation for an extended stay. As more people arrived and the camp swelled to several hundreds, the meetings would often take on a carnivalesque atmosphere. Indeed, some were attracted simply because of the entertainment value of such gatherings. Most, however, came for the "services," which consisted primarily of nonstop preaching and hymn-singing from morning to night.

Most people believed that these were the outward manifestations of a battle going on between the Devil and the Holy Spirit inside a person's soul. Deeply moved by such experiences, many individuals were inspired to publicly confess their sins and to pledge personal reform in the presence of their neighbors. A special area in front of the preachers' platform, called the "sinner's pen" or "mourner's bench," allowed a public forum for this heartrending activity. By the end of the evening, it was not uncommon to find the pen filled to capacity with dozens of men, women, and children, all weeping inconsolably for their past sins and their present salvation.

The eastern cities of the United States were not wholly immune from the religious enthusiasm emanating from the western frontier, although the evangelism there tended to be more sedate and decorous. Instead of camp meetings, the east coast experienced a series of "crusades," well-financed and professionally organized speaking tours that would often sell out the largest auditoriums and lyceums of the day.

Indeed, out of the Second Great Awakening in the east there emerged the enduring American figure of the professional evangelist—a line of individuals stretching from Charles G. Finney (1792–1875) and Dwight L. Moody (1837–1899), to Billy Sunday (1862–1935), and Aimee Semple McPherson (1890–1944), all the way to Billy Graham and Oral Roberts today. Whether ecstatic or staid, however, evangelists and the revivals they spawned became a recurrent feature of the American religious landscape. This provided yet another potent catalyst for the further diversification of Christianity in the United States.

Sectarianism in Nineteenth-Century America

In contrast to the rise of Evangelical Protestantism, with its rhetoric of pan-denominationalism and cooperation, the early nineteenth century also saw the rise of numerous breakaway Protestant groups or sects. Many of these sects found their origins in the Second Great Awakening, although their leaders took them in directions far afield from the comfortable Evangelicalism that the majority of Americans would embrace during that revival.

Mormons Take Off

Joseph Smith (1806–1844), for example, was a young man in upstate New York who found himself uncomfortably disoriented by the religious revivals in his area. Smith was eventually relieved of his religious doubts after visitations by two "heavenly personages." They warned Smith against committing himself to any brand of Protestantism. In time, other angelic visitors would reveal documents to Smith, claiming to have been compiled by Mormon, the second-to-last descendant of an ancient band of Israelite immigrants to America. According to the Book of Mormon, the risen Jesus had founded his original church not only in Israel, but simultaneously in America as well. It was Joseph Smith's mission, therefore, to reestablish this ancient church in America. To do so, he incorporated the Church of Jesus Christ of Latter-Day Saints—today popularly known as the Mormons.

Adventists Crack the Code

Unlike Joseph Smith, William Miller (1782–1849) embraced the enthusiasm of the Second Great Awakening, interpreting it as a signal for Jesus' imminent Second Coming. Miller believed that he had cracked the symbolic code of the Bible, and confidently announced in print that Jesus would return sometime between March 21, 1843 and March 21, 1844. With this, the would-be prophet soon attracted a group of followers that the newspapers of the day derisively called "Adventist" or "Millerite." When the dates came and went without incident, Miller recalculated a new date: October 21, 1844. When Jesus failed to appear on that day—known to history as the "Great Disappointment"—many of Miller's followers, and even Miller himself, abandoned the movement.

On the Right Path

In 1846, Brigham Young led most of the Mormon Church on a 1,300-mile trek to the Great Salt Lake in Utah, where they established their cities and church. This separated them from other Christian groups and enabled them to practice their unique faith as they wished.

And yet, the Adventist movement in the United States survived nevertheless. Under the firm leadership of the visionary Ellen G. White (1827–1915), at least one offshoot of the original Millerites would eventually achieve denominational status under the name Seventh-Day Adventists. Indeed, millennialism, like revivalism, would become a permanent feature in the American religious landscape. Every new generation in America seems to bring another wave of millennial excitement, and new Adventist sects continue to emerge. The Jehovah's Witnesses and Christian Identity movement are two prominent examples.

The Least You Need to Know

- Modernity emphasized skepticism and critical thinking, as well as a positive attitude toward social and intellectual change, and de-emphasized the importance of divine revelation as a source of knowledge.

- The Enlightenment period could be considered anti-clerical and anti-institutional, painting the Roman Catholic Church as the epitome of medieval irrationalism and supernaturalism.

- By the time the English colonies in America eventually achieved their independence in 1781, religious tolerance had become the norm, although making it the official policy of the new federal government was still hotly debated.

- Pietism was a Protestant movement that sought to place the nonrational and experiential elements of the tradition above overly rationalized doctrinal elements.

- The first "Great Awakening," which derived from a combination of the Pietist message and a renewed interest in millennialism, began roughly around 1720 and peaked in 1740, and the Second Great Awakening, lasting roughly from 1790 to 1840, was especially powerful on the United States' rapidly expanding western frontier.

Christianity in the Twentieth Century

In This Chapter

- The theory of evolution causes a stir
- Fundamentalists lose some ground
- Protestant churches unite!
- Roman Catholicism gets modern, for them
- Russia rediscovers religion

As you will see in this chapter, the Christian tradition undergoes immense changes during the modern period. Modernity clashes with the old premodern Christian worldviews in a multitude of ways, and many of the dilemmas created by this conflict have resulted in yet more diversification of the tradition.

Religious Modernism and Its Problems

The modern period held numerous defining moments for Christianity. One occurred when Christians were forced to confront the implications of

Enlightenment rationalism in the eighteenth century. Another came in the second half of the nineteenth century, and it involved the intersection of two seemingly unrelated issues: Darwin's theory of evolution and textual criticism of the Bible.

Chicken or the Egg?

In 1859, Charles Darwin (1809–1882) published *Origin of Species*, and 12 years later he followed this up with *The Descent of Man*. Both books touched off a virulent debate over the validity of the theory of evolution. The idea that higher life forms such as human beings had evolved from lower forms had, of course, already been discussed for centuries. However, Darwin's scientific approach to the problem, not to mention his careful accumulation of evidence, meant that the theory could no longer be dismissed so lightly. Christians, therefore, had to come to terms with the implications of the theory. This was not an easy task.

Not only did Darwin's theory of evolution propose that human beings had evolved from apes, but—perhaps more importantly—Darwin also suggested that this occurred through the completely automatic process of natural selection. Scant room was left for the hand of God in the process. Moreover, it was also a part of the theory that the process of natural selection required millions of years to work. And yet, the biblical account of creation held that the earth was only a few thousand years old, and that life, with all its diversity, had been created in a matter of days. If the theory of natural selection were true, then Genesis must not be a correct account of life's origins.

It's High Time for the Modernists

This was not the first time in the modern age that the Bible had come under serious scientific scrutiny. Since the early part of the century, literary critics and historians had been attempting to separate fact from myth in the Bible by subjecting it to the same kind of scientific analysis used with any other historical document. Such analysis, called "*higher criticism*," had begun in earnest in the Protestant seminaries of Germany, and by the end of the nineteenth century, it was being practiced by biblical scholars throughout Europe and the United States.

Spread the Word

Higher Criticism of the Bible is the scholarly movement that attempted to separate fact from myth in the Bible by subjugating it to the same kind of scientific analysis used with other historical documents.

Higher criticism was called "higher" to differentiate it from earlier criticism that had simply sought to establish the correct version of a biblical text. Higher criticism, on the other hand, was more interested in the biblical authors—their sources, their theological motivations, and their historical context. The higher critics thus approached the biblical text, not as divinely inspired writings, but as human products of a certain time and place, written for immediate purposes, and intended for different audiences. Ultimately, by denying divine inspiration, higher criticism seemed inevitably to call into question the very authority of the Bible itself.

Not all Christians saw the theory of evolution and higher criticism as a threat. In fact, some Protestants and Catholics saw these two products of science as providing new and exciting ways to approach the Christian faith. Those who adopted this position were called religious *modernists*. Higher criticism of the Bible, the religious modernists argued, demonstrated that early Christianity, while more advanced than the other religions of the Ancient world, was nevertheless a product of its age. In its traditional forms, therefore, Christianity was out of place in the modern world. However, borrowing metaphors from biological evolution, religious modernists also believed Christianity was capable of adaptive growth and was therefore destined to evolve into a form more suited to the modern age.

In terms of Protestantism, religious modernists had a profound impact since they served to upset the delicate balance between modernity and tradition that earlier Evangelical Christianity had attempted to chart.

Fundamentalism in America

Protestants in America found the implications of evolution and higher criticism especially troubling.

These people tended to respond to religious modernism by adopting increasingly more conservative attitudes toward the faith. Especially in the Lutheran and Reformed traditions, there emerged able teachers and theologians who argued for the infallibility of the Scriptures and against such heresies as natural selection.

Spread the Word

Modernists are Christians who see the products of science as providing new and exciting ways to approach the Christian faith. "Modernity" emphasized skepticism and critical thinking, as well as a positive attitude toward social and intellectual change. Modernity also tended to de-emphasize the importance of the transcendent in the world, and insisted on the paramount role of the individual in shaping the future.

At a more popular level, conservative Christianity in late-nineteenth-century America coalesced into what came to be called *Fundamentalism*. Fundamentalism was not a single denomination, but, like Evangelical Protestantism itself, it was a set of beliefs and attitudes that cut across denominational boundaries. In 1910, the essentials of this movement were published in a series of primers collectively called *The Fundamentals*. The primers stressed five basic points of Fundamentalist Christianity:

- The infallibility of Scripture
- The virgin birth of Jesus
- Atonement limited to those selected
- The physical, bodily resurrection of Jesus
- The literal Second Coming of Jesus

With this, evangelical Christianity in the United States was effectively split into three separate camps: religious modernists on the left, Fundamentalists on the right, and a large number in the middle who were sympathetic to neither the liberal nor conservative extremes, and who were forced to mediate between them. In time, the tensions between Fundamentalists and religious modernists threatened to split many denominations apart, including the Baptists, the Presbyterians, and the Methodists.

Several times, the tensions between Fundamentalists and modernists came to a head early in the twentieth century.

Spread the Word

Fundamentalism is not a single denomination, but a set of beliefs and attitudes that cut across denominational boundaries. Fundamentalists stress five basic points: (1) the inerrancy of Scripture; (2) the virgin birth of Jesus; (3) atonement limited to the elect; (4) the physical, bodily resurrection of Jesus; and (5) the literal Second Coming of Jesus.

Was the Biology Teacher Doing His Job?

Fundamentalists found biological evolution particularly repugnant and promoted bills in numerous state legislatures to outlaw its presentation in the public schools. In some southern states, Fundamentalists were remarkably successful in this regard. Indeed, in 1925, a high-school biology teacher named John Scopes was brought to trial for violating a Tennessee statute forbidding the teaching of evolution. What began as a simple civil trial, however, gradually mushroomed into a referendum on the modernist/Fundamentalist debate.

Scope's lawyer, Clarence Darrow (1857–1938), well known for his liberal positions, faced off against the state's prosecutor, William Jennings Bryan (1860–1925), equally well known as a champion of Fundamentalism. The fame of these two men attracted widespread public attention, making the trial a national sensation. And while Bryan easily prevailed in the case—Scopes was fined $100—it was Fundamentalism that ultimately paid the highest price.

Many of the reporters who attended the trial, including the celebrated writer and critic H. L. Mencken, tended to ridicule the earnest Bryan in their news stories. The media in general during this period was hostile to all forms of religious conservatism, and after the trial, the stereotype of the ignorant Fundamentalist standing in the way of progress became a staple in America's newspapers, magazines, and novels. Fundamentalism did not disappear, of course;

rather, the movement lowered its profile in America and turned inward, forming its own vigorous but closed subculture. It would be some 50 years before Fundamentalism would reemerge as a potent force in American culture. By this time, religious modernism would be on the wane and the assumptions of modernity itself were coming under fire.

Protestants Get a Wake-Up Call

Many of the events of the first half of the twentieth century shook the West's confidence in modernity. Technology and progress had seemingly led only to mass death and massive destruction of property. Already by the end of World War I (1914–1918), the optimism of the Enlightenment and the modern exaltation of rationalism and technology had been replaced by a mood of deep pessimism. By the end of World War II (1939–1945), this pessimism bordered on despair, especially after the scope of the Nazi Holocaust became widely known.

Church Membership Ups and Downs

Many American Protestant denominations moved more toward the kind of conservative evangelical Christianity reminiscent of that found in the United States in the early nineteenth century. After World War II, the United States entered a period of prosperity and growth that lasted well into the 1960s, and most Americans sought a simple and stable faith that would complement a middle-class lifestyle, not challenge it. Moreover, the so-called "Cold War" between the Western democracies and Marxist

Russia and China also boosted membership in the churches, as regular church attendance became a mark of "Americanism" and patriotic fervor.

There were, however, limits to this growth. After

> **Bet You Didn't Know**
>
> While the vast majority of Europeans during the postwar period remained nominally Christian, no large-scale revivals ensued, and membership actually began to decline. Indeed, many viewed Christianity as exhausted and impotent in the face of the horrors of modern life and turned instead to new secular philosophies such as existentialism and psychoanalysis as an antidote to modernity.

expanding rapidly for a decade, membership in the mainstream Protestant denominations peaked in 1957 and declined thereafter. The growing conservatism of the churches had, it seems, coincided with the growing conservatism of American culture after World War II. And yet in the late 1950s, buoyed by prosperity and fading memories of the World Wars, American culture began another shift toward liberalism—a shift the churches were slow in following.

By the 1960s, much of the younger generation had actually begun to abandon Christianity altogether. Interest in occult practices and witchcraft grew during this period, as did interest in new religious movements such as Scientology. Many were attracted to the exoticism of such Eastern religious movements as Zen Buddhism, Transcendental Meditation, and the International Society for Krishna Consciousness (the so-called "Hare Krishnas"). And still others adopted "secular" psychological and other therapeutic methods for dealing with their existential concerns. In time, some of these people would return to Christianity, but, overall, Protestantism in America during this period experienced a large and seemingly permanent net loss.

> ### On the Right Path
>
> Zen is a school of Mahayana Buddhism that places its emphasis on meditative exercise rather than scriptural study. It is found predominantly in China, Korea, and Japan; in recent years Zen has become very influential in America and Europe.

Evangelicals Become Allies

In response to the perceived cultural and religious chaos of the 1960s, many moderately conservative Protestants in the United States actively began to build bridges to conservative Christians of all stripes. In the early 1970s, there emerged a loose coalition of right-of-center Evangelicals, Fundamentalists, and other conservative Christian groups. Confronted by the counterculture, the members of the "Evangelical Alliance" came to realize that, despite the historical and theological differences that traditionally divided them, they shared certain core values.

In addition to a Bible-centered spirituality, the Evangelical Alliance agreed upon a social and political agenda centering on family values and a strong national defense against global communism. The Evangelical Alliance was particularly effective in promoting their beliefs through sophisticated use of the electronic media—especially television. Tele-evangelists such as Pat Robertson, Jerry Falwell, Jimmy Swaggert, and Jim Bakker became familiar figures during the late 1970s and 1980s. So pervasive did the evangelical message become that politicians during this period found it necessary at least to pay lip service to evangelical concerns. Despite its influence, however, conservative Christianity never claimed more than 16 percent of the American population, a number that has held steady through the 1980s and early 1990s.

Roman Catholics and Vatican II

Roman Catholicism during the postwar period followed similar trends as the Protestants. Although Roman Catholic growth worldwide was spectacular, support for the Church in Europe and the United States was beginning to decline. Unlike the Protestant Churches, however, the centralized control of the papacy allowed the Roman Catholic Church to take concerted action in response.

In 1959, Pope John XXIII (1881–1963) called for a new church council to serve as a "new Pentecost to renew the energies of the Church." Ironically, the Second Vatican Council embraced many elements of religious modernism to do so, and *aggiornamento* ("updating") became the Council's watchword.

From 1962 to 1965, participants in Vatican II sought to revive lay interest in the Church by reinvigorating the deaconate and lay participation in general. The liturgy was reformed such that Latin was replaced by local languages, and the priest, who traditionally faced the altar, was now required to face the congregation during Mass. The Council also cautiously approved higher criticism and more accessible translations of the Bible.

Perhaps inadvertently, Vatican II encouraged a new openness in the Church and a new willingness on the part of the laity and lower clergy to question their bishops and the rest of the Church hierarchy. The modernist stance of many of the pronouncements approved by Vatican II clashed with the conservative outlook of the majority of bishops who hesitated to institute the reforms. What is more, emboldened by Vatican II, many Catholics began to push for even more radical reforms, calling on the Vatican to reverse longstanding bans on artificial birth control, clerical marriage, homosexuality, and the ordination of women.

The Vatican's tolerance of such dissent, however, was remarkably short-lived. By the late 1960s, the

Church under Pope Paul VI began to take steps to counteract the modernist trend. The papal encyclical (letter) *Humanae Vitae* (1968), for example, reiterated the Church's ban on artificial birth control. Moreover, throughout the 1970s and 1980s, the Vatican actively sought to control or silence liberal

---

On the Right Path

On June 14, 1964, Pope Paul VI flew to Jerusalem to meet the patriarch of Constantinople, Athenagoras I. The meeting between the head of the Roman Catholic Church and the ceremonial head of Orthodox Christianity was a momentous occasion. For over a thousand years, these two branches of Christianity had maintained a hostile separation, and little official communication passed between them. On that day in Jerusalem, however, for the first time in the modern age, the two leaders had consented to open a formal dialogue on the possibility of the reunion of these two branches of the Church. Shortly thereafter, an Orthodox-Catholic commission for dialogue was established. Since that time, the commission has engaged in vigorous discussion, although progress toward union has been slow and painful.

Catholic academics and church leaders who spoke out against the hierarchy.

Women who stir up controversy about abortion

rights and female ordination have also been severely rebuked by the papacy. In turn, such unyielding conservative positions have led to a growing chorus of criticism from disaffected Catholics who condemn the authoritarian methods of the Church. Indeed, while many remain loyal to the Church, the number of people abandoning Catholic Christianity in both the United States and Europe has recently increased.

Orthodox Christianity in Russia

Surprisingly, the one place in Europe today where Christianity is experiencing healthy growth is Russia. Despite the triumph of atheistic Marxism in 1917 and the nearly 70 years of religious persecution that followed, the Russian Orthodox Church survived.

When Mikhail Gorbachev assumed power in 1985, his policies of *perestroika* and *glasnost* were accompanied by a gradual relaxing of political pressure against the Church. By the time the Soviet Union finally dis-

On the Right Path

In Russian, *perestroika* translates to "restructuring," referring to a new policy of economic and governmental reform. *Glasnost* means "publicity," referring to a new policy allowing the freer distribution of news and information as well as open discussions about political and social issues.

integrated in 1989, the Orthodox Church was prepared to launch a Christian renaissance in Russia. In some ways this has been a spectacular success.

Indeed, between 1988 and 1993, it is estimated that more than one third of the Russian population under the age of 30 embraced the Church, and between 40 to 60 percent of Russia's 150 million citizens are now classified as believers. Seminary attendance has also soared as old religious schools are slowly being reopened. Moreover, the number of churches in Moscow grew from 47 in 1991 to 370 in 1997, and $300 million have been spent to rebuild Moscow's Christ the Savior cathedral, destroyed in 1931 by Joseph Stalin.

The rebirth of Russian Orthodoxy has not been without its troubling aspects, however. Some of the Church's critics argue that it is quickly losing its independence from the government, and that it might become as much a political tool as it was under the old tsarist regime. Moreover, after decades of Communist persecution, the emerging Church is now aggressively conservative.

Church leaders do not hesitate to squelch dissent within their ranks, and some Church leaders are actively working to make Orthodoxy the only religious option available in Russia. Recently, for example, new legislation has been introduced into the Russian parliament that seeks not only to reestablish the Russian Orthodox Church, but also to ban from Russia the so-called "ungodly sects" of Protestantism.

For many ordinary Russians, this has proved a surprisingly popular issue. Indeed, even the surviving Communist Party attempted to court Orthodox support by pledging to stem the flood of foreign, non-

Orthodox missionaries into Russia if returned to power. It is still too early to tell, however, how far such religious chauvinism will go, or even if the Russian Orthodox renaissance can survive the fading of the euphoria that accompanied the fall of the Soviet system.

The Least You Need to Know

- A defining moment for Christians in the twentieth century involved the intersection of two seemingly unrelated issues: Darwin's theory of evolution and textual criticism of the Bible.

- The five basic points of Fundamentalist Christianity were (1) the infallibility of Scripture; (2) the virgin birth of Jesus; (3) atonement limited to those selected; (4) the physical, bodily resurrection of Jesus; and (5) the literal Second Coming of Jesus.

- In response to the perceived cultural and religious chaos of the 1960s, many moderately conservative Protestants in the United States actively began to build bridges to other conservative Christians.

- From 1962 to 1965, Vatican II sought to revive interest in the Church by conducting Mass in local languages (instead of Latin), requiring the priests to face the congregation (instead of the altar), and cautiously approving higher criticism and more accessible translations of the Bible.

Chapter 7

The Christian Church in the Americas, Asia, and Africa

In This Chapter

- Christianity goes global
- Latin America blends culture and Christianity
- Missions and the Native American Church
- Slow going in Asia
- Africa's Independents, Neotraditionals, and Catholics
- Christianity's future outlook

Christianity, of course, has long had a presence outside of the West. Since the days of the first apostles, the Christian message was carried far beyond the boundaries of the Mediterranean basin, and, by the Middle Ages, thriving Christian communities could be found in Asia and Africa. However, the most intense Christian missionization began with the modern period.

This is an aspect that we have barely touched as yet, but one that will prove to be just as important for the future development of the tradition as the clash with modernity.

The Globalization of Christianity

With the European discovery of the New World in the fifteenth century, Roman Catholic Christianity quickly spread into the Americas. During the following centuries, Roman Catholic missions continued unabated not only in the Americas, but in Asia and Africa as well. Even while the Protestant Reformation shattered the integrity of Western Christianity in the sixteenth and seventeenth centuries, the Roman Catholic Church established successful missions in Southeast Asia and Africa; and in the New World, much of Canada, Mexico, and Central and South America were converted to Roman Catholicism.

Bet You Didn't Know

By the end of the twentieth century, almost no corner of the globe had not been visited by a Christian mission.

Beginning in the eighteenth century, European and then American Protestants, fired by successive revivals, also began extensive missions. A variety of Protestant denominations developed sophisticated missionary societies, often forming cooperative denominational alliances to do so. Wielding effective bureaucracies and massive financial support, the

Protestant missionary societies would extend Protestant Christianity to most of the non-Western world in the nineteenth century.

Not coincidentally, the Christian missionization of the non-Western world paralleled the rise of colonial empires overseas. Indeed, Western governments often saw Christianization as the quickest way to achieve political and economic domination of non-Christian peoples. Missionaries often worked hand in hand with colonial administrators to effect this domination, convinced as they were that Western control would ultimately benefit "backward" peoples.

Christianization has most often assumed Westernization, and such was the overt attitude of most missionaries. In the wake of World War II, however, the old European colonial empires began to disintegrate and, by the late 1960s, the process of decolonization was substantially completed. In some cases this was an orderly process; in others, it was preceded by bloody wars for independence. However decolonization occurred, the process itself precipitated on the part of newly independent peoples everywhere a thorough reevaluation of all aspects of Western culture—including Christianity. The enduring association of Christianity with Western colonialism thus became a highly charged issue in the non-Western world, and in some cases the practice of Christianity was officially discouraged as indelibly foreign and an obstacle to complete decolonization.

Despite this, however, most non-Western Christians have not rejected the tradition, and indeed, the postcolonial growth of Christianity has been explosive.

Part of the reason for this growth is that non-Western Christians have made concerted efforts to create more indigenous expressions of Christianity. This has meant the creation of new, more localized church institutions, a commitment to training indigenous clergy, and the creation of new symbols and rituals that reflect local cultural contexts.

Christianity in Latin America

Roman Catholic missions to the Americas followed in the wake of the Spanish and Portuguese conquests in the sixteenth century, first in the Caribbean and then shortly after on the Latin American mainland itself. The Spanish encountered a variety of indigenous peoples who manifested a wide spectrum of social development.

In the heartlands of Mexico, Guatemala, and Peru, the Aztecs, Maya, and Inca formed sophisticated urban civilizations that rivaled those in Europe. A myriad of trade routes extended the influence of these high civilizations into the *hinterlands*.

Spread the Word

Hinterland can be a region inland from a coast, remote from urban areas, or just beyond major metropolitan or cultural centers.

Underlying these civilizations was an equally wide variety of religious beliefs and institutions that had developed over the centuries, undisturbed by outside forces. Both *conquistadors* (leaders of the Spanish conquest in the Americas) and Catholic missionaries alike had little desire to understand the intricacies of the cultures they faced. For the former, the priority was to establish political and economic control; for the latter, the priority was to save souls from "the clutches of Satan." Both worked together closely, however, resulting in the rapid devastation of indigenous cultures.

A Blend of Culture and Religion

Despite the vigorous efforts of the Catholic missionaries to uproot indigenous cultures, beliefs, concepts, and symbols have never been completely lost. Many, in fact, were gradually blended into local Catholic practice. In the case of Mexico, for example, one can cite the pilgrimage to Tepeyac Hill in Mexico City. According to legend, an Indian named Juan Diego beheld an apparition of the Virgin Mary there in 1534. As a result of that encounter, Juan Diego's garment was miraculously imprinted with the image of a dark-skinned Virgin Mary. To this day, millions of Catholic faithful journey to see the image at Tepeyac, where it now hangs in a massive basilica built for that purpose.

What the legend of Juan Diego does not tell you is that, long before the Spaniards arrived, Tepeyac Hill had been venerated by the Aztecs as sacred to the goddess Tonantizin ("Our Mother"). Many modern scholars have argued, as many early Catholic missionaries had always suspected, that the veneration of the Virgin of Guadalupe at Tepeyac is in part the survival under a different aspect of an ancient Aztec deity. Such was the case throughout Latin America, where native peoples either consciously or unconsciously sought to preserve something of their religion through the creative appropriation and reinterpretation of Catholic symbols.

The Call for Social Justice

For centuries, Roman Catholicism enjoyed a spiritual monopoly in the Latin New World. With Independence in the nineteenth century, Latin America fragmented into a number of republics, many of which sought to curtail the Church's power. The Creole elite of each republic sought to control the Church, just as the king had in the past. After enjoying 400 years of unquestioned domination in Latin America, the Roman Catholic Church began to falter.

Slowly during the twentieth century, however, the Catholic Church began to rebuild its position in Latin America. Vatican II (see Chapter 6) especially would have a major impact on the Latin American Church.

For centuries, both in the colonial and the republican periods, the Roman Catholic Church in Latin America was essentially a conservative organization, upholding the rights and privileges of the elite. During Vatican II, however, the Council called for increased concern for social justice throughout the world and for greater clerical and lay activism on behalf of the poor.

In Latin America, this call for greater social justice resulted in *Liberation Theology*. For Liberation theologians such as Leonardo Boff and Jon Sobrino, sin is the result not only of personal failings, but of social inequalities. Catholics, therefore, were obliged to fight for social justice as much as they were obliged to fight against personal sin. In some cases, individual priests and nuns actually took part in violent revolutionary movements.

Spread the Word

Liberation Theology is a twentieth-century theological movement within Roman Catholicism. According to Liberation Theology, sin is the result not only of personal failings, but of social inequalities. Catholics, therefore, are obligated to fight for social justice as much as they are obligated to fight against personal sin.

Mostly, though, the Church began to pursue social justice in Latin America in less radical ways. For example, through a series of Bishops' Conferences in the 1970s and 1980s, Latin American Church leaders devised long-term strategies to shift the emphasis of pastoral work more toward the economically and politically oppressed in the Americas. Ultimately, Liberation Theology came to have a powerful impact, not only in Latin America, but in the Philippines and South Africa as well.

The Rise of Pentecostalism

After 500 years of Roman Catholic influence, it is not surprising to find that today some 91.8 percent of the population of Latin America at least nominally identify themselves as Catholics. However, this number is now gradually beginning to decline as more and more Latin Americans have turned to Protestantism. Perhaps the most spectacular growth among Protestant groups is that of *Pentecostalism*, a Protestant sectarian movement that stresses the importance of individual possession by the Holy Spirit. Pentecostalism arose in the United States during the first decade of this century. It then spread rapidly both throughout North America and the Caribbean, and, in recent decades, throughout the rest of Latin America. Today, Pentecostalism claims about 70 percent of the estimated 18 million Protestants in Latin America.

 Spread the Word

Pentecostalism is a religious movement within Protestantism that began in the United States in the early twentieth century. It emphasized spontaneous participation in worship and immediate experience of the Holy Spirit.

Pentecostals in Latin America tend to be from the lower economic classes, day laborers, and the unemployed. Many are attracted to the Pentecostal emphasis on spontaneous participation in worship and immediate religious experiences such as speaking in tongues. One of the important reasons for Pentecostal growth is the fact that it relies on a largely lay ministry—anyone touched by the Holy Spirit can minister. For this reason, Pentecostalism spontaneously develops its own indigenous clergy. Moreover, despite the fact that there is some outside financial support (primarily from the United States), Pentecostal groups tend to be small, austere, and largely self-supporting.

Some have cited the possible coming together of elements of Pentecostalism to account for its popularity. To religious studies scholars, the fact that Pentecostalism emphasizes spirit possession, faith healing, and the belief in evil spirits seems to suggest that it is continuous with indigenous Amerindian and African traditions. This may be the case, but Pentecostals tend to be very orthodox Christians in terms of their ritual practices and symbolism. There are, however, long-established Christian traditions in Latin America that are openly intermingled.

Christian Missions to Native Americans in North America

Often ignored in discussions of non-Western Christianity is Christianity among the Native peoples of North America. Throughout the colonial period, Native Americans were the target of Spanish, French, and English missionary efforts. With the creation of the United States, the Federal government often used Christian missionaries as Indian agents and allowed them a great deal of influence over Indian affairs. The Federal government employed both Roman Catholics and Protestants in this capacity.

> ### Divine Inspiration
>
> In the Caribbean there are multiple examples of traditions that blend Catholic Christianity with traditional African religious ideas and symbols. Cuban Santerìa, for example, is a blend of Yoruba (West African) religious beliefs and Catholicism. Haitian Voodoo represents a blending of Nigerian, Beninian, and Zairian deities and the cult of saints found in Roman Catholicism. Likewise, Shango (Trinidad), Winti (Surinam), and Umbanda (Brazil) are also vigorous syncretic Christianities. In each of these traditions there is an emphasis on spirit possession, shamanism, and faith healing, and each now finds part of its membership outside of its country of origin.

Today, almost no Native American tribe has been untouched by Christianity, although there have been varying degrees of acceptance. One of the earliest missionized peoples of North America, the Pueblos of the southwest, strongly resisted the inroads of the Franciscan missionaries in the seventeenth century. In fact, at one point, the Pueblos revolted against Spanish control and forced conversion, and managed to hold the Spanish at bay for decades. Even after the Spanish had reestablished control, the Pueblos continued practicing their tribal religion in secret even while practicing Catholic Christianity in public.

Indian-Style Christianity

On the other hand, other Native American tribes have embraced Christianity so that today they practice little of their traditional religion. The Yaqui of Arizona and the Cherokee of Georgia, for example, adopted Christianity *en masse* during the colonial period. Most tribes, however, were converted one individual at a time, and only over several generations did an entire tribe shift in its primary religious identification.

It is perhaps partly for this reason that, even today, when increased respect has led to a renaissance of tribal religions, many Native Americans have decided to remain Christians. Indeed, perhaps the most well-known Native American religious figure—Black Elk (c. 1863–1950)—spent the majority of his life as a Catholic missionary. Today, a high percentage of Native Americans identify themselves primarily as Christian.

Native Americans have also confronted the challenges of Christianization in much more creative ways than simple rejection or acceptance. A high degree of blending of Christian symbolism with the Native American symbols and practices can be found in many new religious movements among Native Americans, from the colonial period to the present.

The Longhouse religion of the Iroquois, for example, developed from the *Gaiwiio* ("Good News") revealed to a charismatic Seneca named Handsome Lake (1735–1815).

The Ghost Dance movement, which was to have such tragic consequences for the Sioux Indians at Wounded Knee in 1890, actually began a decade earlier with a Paiute named Wovoka who claimed the dance itself had been revealed to him by a distinctly Jesus-like figure.

Native American Church

Perhaps the most dynamic Native American new religion is the Native American Church, which has both its Christian and non-Christian forms. The Native American Church centers on the ritual use of *peyote*. For centuries, Indians of northern Mexico used peyote as part of their complex religious rites. In the nineteenth century, the ritual use of peyote spread to the United States where it was formally organized into the Native American Church.

Despite concerted efforts at suppression by the U.S. government, the new movement has thrived and has served as one means by which Native Americans have united across tribal boundaries. Interestingly, many local congregations have endeavored to incorporate elements of Christianity into their practices. The use of peyote is often compared to the Christian sacrament of the Eucharist, for example, and the spirit of the peyote is often identified with Jesus. Bible readings are also a common feature of peyote ceremonies.

What is truly remarkable about such blended congregations is that they are fully accepted by the Native American Church at large. Such Christ-centered congregations are considered simply one more tribal variation among many within the movement.

Bet You Didn't Know

Peyote (pronounced *pay-o-tee*) is a type of spineless cactus that, when ingested, typically through smoking like tobacco leaves, has mild hallucinogenic effects.

Christianity in Asia

Asia has felt the least Christian influence of the three regions we are considering in this chapter, and Christians comprise, on average, only 3.5 percent of the population of each country in Asia. Nevertheless, given the massive population of the region, Asians still account for 10 percent of the world population of Christians. Nestorian Christians first established themselves in China as early as the seventh century, and their church lasted for some two centuries. In the fourteenth century, there was renewed Christian interest in China when a Franciscan mission journeyed to Beijing in a failed effort to convert the Khubla Khan.

In the sixteenth century, Spain took control of the Philippine archipelago and the Philippines became a staunchly Catholic country. During the sixteenth and seventeenth centuries, the Jesuits missionized both China and Japan and, for a time, enjoyed some success in founding small congregations in both countries. Francis Xavier's work (1506–1552), for example, enjoyed considerable success in Japan until persecution slowed Christianity's growth in 1597.

Colonial Expansion Helps

Again, it was not until the massive colonial expansion of the West in the nineteenth century that Christianity began to make considerable headway in Asia outside the Philippines. After the Opium Wars of 1840 allowed the Western powers to gain a colonial foothold in China, Roman Catholic and Protestant missionaries from both Europe and the United States established themselves in almost every province of China.

Bet You Didn't Know

Officially atheistic, the government has allowed churches to operate only under the most stringent conditions, and persecution of clergy and of members continues to this day. Today, there are an estimated three to five million Christians in China.

Despite the resources lavished on China, and despite the long-term presence of Western missionaries, growth was slow, and only a few congregations managed to root themselves permanently in Chinese soil. Things were made considerably more difficult for Christian expansion after the Chinese Revolution brought the communists to power in 1949.

In other areas, Christian gains have been marginal at best, slowed by both political and cultural obstacles. Perhaps in all cases in Asia, with the possible exception of the Philippines, the unevenness in the growth of Christianity has been due to its foreignness and indelible association with Western imperialism. Ironically, precisely because of its foreign origin, Christianity has functioned as a religion of protest in some Asian countries. Korea is an interesting example in this regard. Throughout the early modern period, Korea resisted both Western and Christian influence. Ultimately, however, Korea was colonized by a non-Western power, Japan. Throughout the period of Japanese occupation (1910–1945), Presbyterian and Methodist missionaries made great strides, bringing in millions of Korean converts. Why? Perhaps Buddhism was too closely associated with Korea's colonial oppressors, the Japanese. Christianity, while a foreign tradition, nevertheless functioned well as a religion of protest against Japanese influence. Today, there are more than 14 million Christians in Korea.

Again, the combination of religions has been a factor in the growth of Christianity in Asia. The T'ai P'ing rebellion of Hung-hsiu Ch'üan (1813–1864), for example, employed amalgams of Christian, Taoist, and Buddhist symbolism. More recently, in Vietnam, we find Caodaism, a blend of Buddhism, Taoism, and Roman Catholicism.

The Unification "Moonies"

Perhaps the most interesting, and definitely the most successful, contemporary blended religious movement has been the Unification Church, originating in Korea. The Unification Church was founded in 1954 by the Reverend Sun Myung Moon (b. 1920). Years earlier, on Easter Day, 1936, Moon claimed that Jesus appeared to him and asked him to assume responsibility for the establishing of the Kingdom of God on Earth. Over the succeeding decades, Moon also communicated with a variety of other religious leaders such as the Buddha and Moses, and on one occasion, God himself.

Drawing on the insights of these meetings, Moon developed a body of religious teaching, published as the *Divine Principle*. In it, Moon set forth a messianic, millennial religion dedicated to the unification of the world in anticipation of the establishment of the Kingdom of God. So popular did Moon's message become, and so effective was he in promoting it, that by the end of the 1960s Moon commanded a global religious movement, known as Tong II in Korea and the Unification Church in the West. By the 1970s, the "Moonies" claimed a membership of 30,000, in which 5,000 were in the United States alone.

Christianity in Africa

One of the earliest national Christian churches in the world was African. According to legend, the Ethiopian Church was founded by Syrian missionaries early in the fourth century and has survived to the present day. Despite this fact, throughout much of Africa's history, Christianity has had a limited impact.

The rise of Islam in the seventh century over-whelmed the traditional Christian churches of North Africa. Islam quickly became the majority religion of most of northern Africa. Sub-Saharan Africa, on the other hand, remained unmissionized both by Islam and by Christianity. Part of this was due to the strength of indigenous religious traditions that continue strong to this day. Another factor was the rise of the slave trade, which was promoted in part by both Islamic and Christian slave traders.

To convert large portions of Sub-Saharan Africa meant removing a large portion of the population as potential targets for slavery. It made more economic sense and reduced the ethical qualms of both Muslims and Christians if only "pagans" were enslaved. Only Portuguese Catholics made any concerted efforts to evangelize Africans. They maintained missions on the west coast of Africa from the sixteenth to the eighteenth century, but they achieved little lasting impact.

With the demise of the global slave trade in the eighteenth and nineteenth centuries, this situation gradually began to change in Sub-Saharan Africa. At this point, Islamic leaders had neither the political interest nor the resources to missionize Sub-Saharan Africa. Islam had a hard enough time maintaining its position within its heartlands because of the pressure of Western colonialism. The West, on the other hand, had both the political will and the resources to support the Christianization of Africa, and large-scale missionization began in the early nineteenth century.

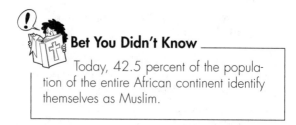

Bet You Didn't Know

Today, 42.5 percent of the population of the entire African continent identify themselves as Muslim.

Such missionization was at first largely a Protestant affair. In 1827, for example, the Anglican- and Methodist-funded Fourah Bay College was founded in Sierra Leone as a seminary for black Africans. Over the years, it produced a series of locally prominent clergymen and missionaries who firmly established a network of Christian communities on the west coast of Africa. Most Western missionization, however, remained in the hands of white missionaries.

Arriving in Africa in the hundreds if not thousands by the 1890s, most worked tirelessly to build churches, schools, and hospitals, and to translate the Bible into the myriad of local languages. In time, too, the Roman Catholic Church revived its missionary efforts in Africa, and, if the nineteenth and early twentieth centuries were the golden age of Protestant missionization, then the second half of the twentieth century has been the golden age for Catholic missions in Africa. Today, it is the largest denomination in almost all countries in Africa. All told, there is now an aggregate Christian population of more than 150 million people in Africa, with Christians forming the majority of the population in countries as diverse as Zaire, Ghana, Togo, Uganda, Zimbabwe, Namibia, Angola, and South Africa.

The Independent Churches

Part of the phenomenal growth of Christianity in Africa is due to the presence of a vigorous African independent church movement whose roots go back to the nineteenth century. Most of these groups have arisen in part as an attempt to regain the political, economic, and psychological control lost to Western colonialism. Some of the churches within the independent movement represent schisms from the established missions of the Anglican, Methodist, Presbyterian, and Baptist denominations. Most of the schismatic independents have retained the liturgy and church structure of their parent groups. Primarily at issue in these schisms were the lack of African control and promotion through the hierarchy, as well as the acute problem of inculturation.

One such movement was the incredibly popular East African Revival or Balokole ("the Saved"). Breaking away from the Anglican Mission in Rwanda in the 1930s, the Revival subsequently developed a modified Anglican liturgy and a village-based organizational structure. Nor has Roman Catholicism been wholly immune from this tendency toward greater African control through schism. The Franciscan Pleaide Tempels (b. 1906) founded a movement called *Jamaa* (Swahili word for "family") in Zaire. By 1953, it had become substantially independent from the Catholic Church. Although orthodox in terms of its Catholicism, *Jamaa* nevertheless stresses the importance of local control. Similar Catholic breakaways have formed in Kenya (the Legion of Mary) and in Zambia (the Catholic Church of the Sacred Heart).

Bet You Didn't Know

The leaders of the schismatic independent movements chose the labels of "African" or "Ethiopian" to symbolize the fact that their movements were self-conscious attempts to create a kind of Protestant Christianity appropriate to Africa.

In addition to breakaway churches from the mainstream denominations, other churches have formed from the influence of smaller Christian sects, many from the United States. A whole series of independent "Zionist" churches in South Africa, for example, trace their roots to the missionary work of the Evangelical Christian Catholic Church, founded by John Alexander Dowie in 1896 in Zion City, Illinois. The most widespread movement in Sub-Saharan Africa, the Church of the Watchtower or Kitawala, traces its roots back to the first missionaries of the Jehovah's Witnesses who arrived in Africa early in this century. The strong millennialism of the Kitawala has excited many, and today, Watchtower groups can be found throughout central and southern Africa.

The independent church movement in Africa also has its more grassroots manifestations. Such movements tend to center on the leadership of local charismatic prophets and place an emphasis on faith healing. Perhaps the most famous example of such an independent church was that which formed in the wake of the prophetic career of William Wade Harris (1865–1929), a Liberian school teacher.

Harris, nominally a Methodist, experienced a series of visions in which the Angel Gabriel commanded him to proselytize the west coast of Africa. Adopting an ascetic lifestyle, Harris became a wandering faith healer and evangelist, preaching a simple Christian monotheism and promising his listeners a better life if they were to abandon their "pagan idols" and traditional practices. After a year of preaching, Harris had succeeded in baptizing thousands, and, despite the fact that Harris founded no church, a "Harrist" Church nevertheless spontaneously arose and exists to this day.

On the Right Path

Harris's prophetic career became the model for countless other prophetic movements that have arisen subsequently throughout Africa in the twentieth century, such as the Kimbanguist Church in Zaire, the Aladura ("people of prayer") Church in Nigeria, and the Lumpa Church of Zambia. Several other such grassroots independent churches could be cited, and in many of them, the prophetic founder is identified as the new messiah and herald of the millennium. Even now, new independent churches still arise, adding continually to the diversity of homegrown African Christianity.

The Neotraditional Churches

In many cases, the problem with Western missionary Christianity was not so much the lack of indigenous leadership, but the lack of respect for traditional beliefs and practices manifested by the missions. Thus, we find arising a number of independent churches that, in addition to responding to charismatic leadership, also strive to create a harmonious blend between indigenous religious symbols and Christian symbols.

In these neotraditional churches, such beliefs and practices as ancestor worship, food taboos, the belief in witchcraft, and, in some cases, polygamy, have all been preserved and integrated into a Christian context. The most successful examples of such neotraditionalist churches include Église de Dieu de Nos Ancêtres (Church of the God of Our Ancestors) in Zaire and the Église des Banzie (Church of the Initiates) in Gabon. Many more neotraditionalist churches have arisen spontaneously in villages and cities throughout Africa and, because of the highly local nature of the beliefs and practices being preserved, have remained local in outreach.

Ironically, in many cases the syncretic process involved in the creation of these neotraditionalist groups was facilitated by the ready availability of the Bible in translation. Written in a cultural milieu closer to that of the rural African than that of the Western missionary, the Bible was also taken more literally by the average rural African. The visions, dreams, miracles, magic, and witchcraft with which the Old and New Testaments abound did not have to be allegorized away, but were accepted as corollaries of local beliefs and practices.

Even a practice as repugnant to Westerners as polygamy finds ample precedent in the Old Testament examples of David and Solomon. Despite decades of Western missionary discouragement, the neotraditional independent churches have only to appeal to the authority of the Bible itself to counter Western claims of syncretism. Indeed, the premodern world of non-Western peoples is much closer to that of the authors of the Bible than that of Western missionaries whose worldview actually represents a compromise between modernity and Christianity.

The Catholic Church

On the outskirts of the city of Yamoussoukro, the administrative capital of the West African country of the Ivory Coast, rises majestically the largest church in the world—the Roman Catholic Basilica of Our Lady of Peace. Built in post-Renaissance style, the basilica is 623 feet long and its dome reaches 525 feet above the ground—making it some 100 feet higher than St. Peter's Basilica in Rome. The entire basilica complex is preceded by a 7.4-acre esplanade paved in Italian marble, partially enclosed by rows of 128 Doric columns, each standing 84 feet high and 10 feet wide.

Some 300,000 people would fit in the esplanade's plaza, and the basilica itself accommodates 7,000 worshipers inside. Built in less than four years by an army of 1,450 skilled artisans, the basilica was said to have cost between $100 and $200 million. The late Felix Houphouët-Boignet, president of Ivory Coast and initiator of the project, built the basilica as a gift to the Vatican and expressed the hope that it would become a pilgrimage destination not only for African Catholics, but for Christians throughout the world.

Although finding the world's largest church in Africa may seem surprising, it is symbolic of a fundamental fact about Christianity as it approaches its third millennium: For the first time in over a thousand years, the majority of the world's Christians are not of European origins. Christianity no longer finds its heartland in the West. As one observer commented recently, "By the middle of the next century … Christianity as a world religion will patently have its centre of gravity in the Equatorial and Southern latitudes, and every major denomination, except possibly the Orthodox Church, will be bound to regard those areas as its heartlands …."

The Basilica of Our Lady is, however, an ambiguous symbol. For, despite its African location and the nationality of its patron, the basilica nevertheless reflects the continuing control the West exercises over non-Western Christianity. The basilica, for example, is staffed entirely with clergy from Poland, and most of its operating costs are funded by Western sources. Perhaps even more telling is the fact that the basilica's architecture is straight out of the Western tradition, its liturgy incorporates few local ritual forms, and, among the numerous figures that appear in the basilica's 36 immense stained-glass windows, only one is black.

On the Right Path

> Today, fully 6 out of every 10 Christians are found outside Europe and the United States. The fact that the largest church in the world is now no longer found in the West is fitting, therefore, since the largest population of Christians is no longer found in the West.

The Future of Global Christianity

As it enters its third millennium, Christianity is now poised to be a truly global religion. What might this mean for the tradition as a whole? It is hard to say, of course, but the next few decades will be decisive in determining the tradition's future course. As suggested in this chapter, perhaps the greatest challenge for the tradition is to be found in the evolving relationship between Western and non-Western Christians. As we have seen, despite decolonization, Westerners nevertheless still continue to influence and, to a certain degree, control the destinies of non-Western Christianities.

Many postcolonial churches still use the European languages of their colonizers, and theology and liturgy are still largely dependent on Western theological and philosophical vocabularies. In addition, the highest leadership roles tend to be in the hands of Westerners. This is likely to continue for a variety of reasons. The majority of Church members outside the West are predominantly poor, young (42 percent of the population of the Third World is under 15), and lacking in educational opportunities.

 On the Right Path

Early Western missionaries working in Latin America, Asia, and Africa often discouraged local productions using indigenous motifs, techniques, and materials, seeking instead to impose Western aesthetic values when it came to religious art. As we can see with the Basilica of Our Lady in the Ivory Coast, such attitudes have not wholly disappeared today. Nevertheless, today, with the increasing awareness of the subjectivity and ethnocentric bias that goes into the creation of aesthetic judgments, there has been an increasing willingness by Western Christians to accept culturally different presentations of Christian symbols and, taken on its own terms, an increasing appreciation for the intrinsic beauty of this religious art.

There is, however, a growing awareness among the historic denominations that Western domination is driving members away from the mainstream Christian denominations. In Latin America, the leaders of Roman Catholicism see thousands of their members leave the church every year for alternatives such as Pentecostalism, which offers more local control and participation. In Africa, it is said that, annually, up to 450,000 leave both Catholic and Protestant denominations to become members of the growing Independent Church movement, which is adding some 100 new denominations every year.

In response, the historic denominations have made great strides to produce indigenous clergy and to promote non-Westerners through the denominational hierarchies. Within the Roman Catholic Church, for example, the number of Asian and African bishops has increased from 33 in 1951 to more than 700 today. Similar statistics can be cited for many of the historic Protestant denominations as well.

Nevertheless, the growth of the new churches outside the West has been as much a response to the desire for *acculturation* as it has been for administrative control. As we have seen in this chapter, there has been a great desire to harmonize Christianity with local beliefs and practices. Since Christianity historically has tended to stress orthodoxy and orthopraxy, diversification, whether through doctrinal development or through *syncretism*, has always been vigorously resisted. Even today, the leadership of the Western denominations has continued to have a limited toleration for acculturation, fearing that it will ultimately lead to syncretism.

Spread the Word

Acculturation is the cultural modification of an individual, group, or people by adapting to or borrowing traits from another culture. **Syncretism** is the combination of different forms of belief or practice.

Despite Vatican II's call for greater indigenization of Catholicism, for example, the Roman Catholic archbishop of Lusaka, Emmanuel Milingo, was forced to resign after charges of syncretism in 1982. After two millennia of striving for strict orthodoxy, therefore, it is doubtful that the Western denominations will abandon their conservatism anytime soon.

Does this mean that a permanent rift is now developing between Western and non-Western Christianity, like that which poisoned relations between the Roman Catholic and the Eastern Orthodox Churches? Surprisingly, probably not. As mentioned in Chapter 3, the desire for the global unity of Christianity has always been strong. At no time has that desire for unity been stronger than today.

Ever since the beginning of this century, the realization that Western society was becoming increasingly secularized and materialistic led to calls for wider cooperation and perhaps reunion between the Western denominations. Such a spirit of *ecumenism* ("one worldism") has, in recent years, led to much hopeful dialogue. In time, however, the ever-growing secularity not only of the West, but also of the rest of the planet as well, will probably force Western Christians to come to an understanding not only with other Western Christians, but with Christians everywhere, regardless of their cultural backgrounds. In this way, faced with the competition of another rapidly globalizing worldview—modernity—the Christian tradition will finally be forced to embrace diversity, not flee from it.

> ### Spread the Word
>
> **Ecumenicism** is an ongoing move-
> ment that encourages the worldwide
> reunion and cooperation of the Christian
> churches.

The creation of new forms of Christianity, of
course, has not been an easy task. As the Basilica of
Our Lady suggests, the Western cultural context out
of which Christianity emerged is difficult to shake.
Moreover, the leadership of the major Christian
denominations still resides in the West, and most
are highly resistant to local control. Nevertheless,
the process of creating new non-Western forms of
Christianity is proceeding quickly. In some cases, it
is occurring within traditional denominational
structures; in other cases, new breakaway forms of
Christianity are arising, many of which are syncretic
blends of indigenous beliefs and practices. In all
cases, the centuries-old process of Christian diversification is accelerating even more.

The Least You Need to Know

- The postcolonial growth of Christianity has
  been explosive, partly because non-Western
  Christians have made concerted efforts to
  create new, localized church institutions and
  develop new symbols and rituals that reflect
  local cultural contexts.

- After 500 years of Roman Catholic influence, it is not surprising to find that today some 91.8 percent of the population of Latin America at least nominally identifies itself as Catholic.

- The most dynamic new Native American religion is the Native American Church, which has both its Christian and non-Christian forms, centering on the ritual use of peyote.

- Perhaps the most interesting, and definitely the most successful, contemporary blended religious movement in Asia has been the Unification Church (also known as the "Moonies") originating in Korea, founded in 1954 by the Reverend Sun Myung Moon.

- The Independent, Neotraditional, and Catholic Churches all play a role in African Christianity and cultural beliefs and practice.

- The process of creating new non-Western forms of Christianity is proceeding quickly.

Chapter 8

Christian Beliefs in a Postmodern Age

In This Chapter

- Postmodernity becomes popular
- Belief in God and Jesus
- Do sinners go to heaven or hell?
- Devil on the left; angel on the right

In this chapter, we will explore some of the ways in which "postmodernity" is impacting Christianity, especially in terms of its traditional beliefs.

Along Comes Postmodern Christianity

At the beginning of the twentieth century, some scholars began to speculate that in the face of modernity, most people in the West would gradually abandon religion, creating as they did increasingly secular societies. In other words, the worldview of modernity would eventually come to wholly replace the premodern worldviews as embodied in Christianity.

As we near the end of the century, however, we can see that this process of secularization has not proceeded as predicted. Institutional Christianity in the West has indeed declined. Church membership and attendance have fallen, fewer people are choosing to marry in church, the number of clergy is declining, and elementary religious education for children is at an all-time low. And yet, this is not because people in the West have abandoned premodern worldviews. In fact, public opinion polls seem to indicate that people in the West are as spiritual as they have ever been. Moreover, while Christian institutions falter, Christian concepts and symbols still permeate Western culture to a high degree. How can we account for this?

What seems to be occurring in Christianity in the West is that large sectors of the society no longer feel compelled to make a hard and fast choice between the modern and premodern worldviews. Critical of the failures of modernity on the one hand, but aware of some of the limitations of premodern worldviews on the other, individuals now seek to live their lives by balancing aspects of both worldviews. Of course, such a balancing act requires a high degree of intellectual flexibility, spontaneity, and willingness to compromise.

Since flexibility and spontaneity are not the values of the institutional churches, especially those that insist on a strict orthodoxy, many individuals have begun to turn away from the churches. Increasingly, therefore, religion has come to be seen as a private affair in the West. Thus, while the institutional churches steadily lose members, this does not mean that the West is becoming more secular or even less Christian. It simply means that Christianity itself is being privatized and deinstitutionalized.

Scholars have labeled the general trend toward the conscious blending of premodern and modern world-views "postmodern," and therefore the religious balancing act we are witnessing in today's society can properly be called "postmodern" Christianity.

The "Popular" Religion

In some ways, postmodern Christianity is simply a new version of popular Christianity. Every "official" religion has its "popular" variants. In general, popular religion is the product of people who have little contact with the institutional churches, little religious training, and who get their religious information through informal channels. Scholars have noted that even without formal religious education, most people will devise rudimentary religious systems, taking ideas and practices where they find them, and using them to deal with the existential problems of every-day life.

Such has been the case with popular forms of Christianity throughout the ages. For centuries, the majority of people living in Christian countries received little or no formal religious education or had little connection with the institutional churches. And yet, such people managed to create for themselves workable, if highly idiosyncratic, versions of Christianity.

> **Divine Inspiration** _____
>
> "Popular" religious systems may not be absolutely coherent intellectually, but if a person believes that it aids in the production of food or wealth, or heals physical or psychological illness, then it is likely to thrive.

In many cases, unhampered by official concerns for doctrinal purity, such popular Christianities have been highly syncretic, combining folk beliefs and practices with those of orthodox Christianity. In some cases, as we have seen, these syncretic beliefs and practices have been tolerated or adopted by the institutional churches (for example, the cult of saints and pilgrimage). But in most cases, since popular Christianity was found largely among the poor and illiterate, the typical response by the institutional churches was simply to ignore its existence.

Today, however, the situation in the West is radically different, for while postmodern Christianity shares some important characteristics with the popular Christianity of the past, there are some crucial differences between the two. Like popular Christianity, postmodern Christianity tends to be highly idiosyncratic, intensely pragmatic, and willingly syncretic, even to the point of openly denying Christian uniqueness. However, unlike popular Christianity, postmodern Christianity is the province of all sectors of society, not just the poor and marginalized.

The Downfall of Modernity

The challenge of modernity and its later collapse forced everyone in Western society to reassess their beliefs. Even the rich and powerful, who traditionally had the most to gain by supporting the institutional churches, felt compelled to criticize the rigid premodern worldview of institutional Christianity. They, too, began to forge religious paths independent of the institutional churches. What this means for today is that postmodern Christianity is now found among all social classes in both rural and urban settings. Because of this, postmodern Christianity is beginning to exert an influence over institutional Christianity in ways that the popular Christianity of the past never could.

It must be emphasized, however, that postmodern Christianity is by its very nature a plural phenomenon: There is no *one* postmodern Christian tradition. In this chapter, we will attempt to come to terms with postmodern Christianity in the West by contrasting a wide range of postmodern beliefs with those "official" beliefs espoused by the institutional churches. As we do so, we shall also explore how the tensions between postmodern and official beliefs (as well as the practices from Chapter 9) are slowly transforming the Christian tradition as a whole.

Christian Beliefs in the Postmodern West

Recent public opinion polls conducted in the United States have repeatedly indicated that a vast majority of all Americans believe that religion is an important part of life. This is not an unexpected finding, since the population of the United States has always shown a high degree of religious commitment.

What was unusual about the poll is that it also revealed that an almost equally large majority felt that you should determine your own religious beliefs independently of organized religion. Indeed, for those who did participate in organized religion, few knew their denomination's stand on many doctrinal issues or even what doctrinal issues set their denomination apart from other denominations.

Belief in God

At the beginning of the 1990s, 94 percent of all Americans said they believed in God. A majority of these people claimed that they were occasionally very aware of the presence of God in their lives, experienced divine guidance, and were actively seeking a closer relationship to God. Like the United States, the rest of the West also still believes in God, although not as emphatically so.

Perhaps as striking as the erosion of belief in God is the erosion of any consensus among believers on how God should be conceptualized. For most "official" Christianity in the West, the nature of divinity had been comprehensively defined by the doctrine of the Trinity, which sought to create an identity between God, Jesus, and the Holy Spirit. This, however, was always difficult to picture.

Popular Christianity tended to explode this synthesis in order to create a more logical and simple conception of the deity as the gray-bearded old man, familiar from Michaelangelo's painting on the ceiling of the Sistine Chapel. Postmodern Christianity, too, has largely rejected the notion of the Trinity, but it has failed to produce any one overwhelmingly popular alternative picture.

Bet You Didn't Know

In the face of modernity, belief in God in Western countries has steadily eroded over the decades, and today there is a greater toleration for agnosticism and atheism throughout the West. Among Americans, six in seven people say that individuals have the right not to believe in God if they wish.

In Western Europe, only about half the population who believe in God think of the concept in anthropomorphic terms (as having human form). The other half see God simply as an idea of goodness or as the spirit behind the laws of nature. Some even resort to other religions' concepts of divinity in order to conceive of God. Thus he becomes the impersonal Tao of Taoism or the attribute-less Brahman of Vedantic Hinduism. Today, it is impossible to make any generalization about a generic Western concept of God.

Even in the United States, where a higher percentage of people believe in a personal God than anywhere else in the West, there is nevertheless no consensus on how this personal God should be conceptualized. Especially thorny is the question of the gender of God. In the past, both official and popular Christianity conceived of God as exclusively male, despite some passages in the Bible that suggest a more androgynous nature.

Today, however, even institutional Christianity is now taking God's androgyny more seriously. In 1983, for example, the National Council of Churches issued a gender-neutral reading of the Bible. This translation is careful to refer to God as the "Heavenly Parent" in an attempt to counteract the tendency to imagine God as exclusively male.

On the Right Path

In order to signify a more androgynous God, a recent gender-inclusive translation of the Bible renders the familiar beginning lines of the Lord's Prayer ("Our Father who art in heaven …") as "God, our Father and Mother, who is in the heavens …."

And yet, not all are comfortable with this trend, fearing that such translations endanger "the divinely ordained uniqueness of men and women." In 1997, bowing to the pressures of conservative Evangelicals, the International Bible Society, the largest publisher of Bibles in the United States, dropped its plans for what they called a "gender-accurate" translation of the Bible. This, in turn, invited criticism from more liberal Christians. Feminist theologians, for example, have been arguing for decades that the sexism of the Bible was a product of the ancient times in which the Bible was recorded, and not inherent in the biblical message itself.

Indeed, for them, the sexist language of the Bible is the starting point for an all-encompassing critique of traditional Christian patriarchy. Both sides, therefore, see changes in biblical language as a potential catalyst for large-scale change in the Christian tradition.

Belief in Jesus

When we come to the significance of Jesus, however, we do not find the same kind of unanimity. According to official Christianity, Jesus was sent by God to redeem people from their sins and to reconcile them with God so that they may be saved from death at the Last Judgment.

Jesus is said to have accomplished this in two ways. First, Jesus was a human being who, through his life and ministry, presented humanity with a model for a perfect life that made it doubly possible for each individual to achieve salvation. Second, it is taught that Jesus was God himself, whose suffering and death on the cross was a divine sacrifice that overcame the inherent sinfulness of the world and made possible the salvation of all humanity.

In the past, popular Christianity tended to exalt Jesus' divine nature above his humanity, but during the modern period the trend seemed to be reversed: His humanity and his role as ethical teacher were celebrated. What is more, among those who see Jesus as simply a great ethical teacher, there is a decreased tendency to see him as the *greatest* ethical teacher. Many Europeans now see Jesus as on a par with Mohammed or the Buddha, thus blunting any claim to the uniqueness of Christian ethical insights or to Western moral superiority in general.

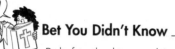

Bet You Didn't Know

Belief in the historical Jesus seems to be secure in the West. An overwhelming 93 percent of all Americans did not doubt the historical existence of Jesus in 1996, nor do the majority of Western Europeans.

The Nature and Destiny of Humanity

As in other world religions, salvation in Christianity is ultimately a promise of life after death.

Do You Have Original Sin?

The Christian churches teach that the human soul is immortal, and was originally destined to spend eternity in the presence of God in heaven. However, according to Christian teachings, the first human beings, Adam and Eve, rebelled against the will of God, thus jeopardizing their life of eternal happiness.

Due to this "original sin," which all humans share, all human beings are naturally inclined to disobey the will of God. Jesus' death on the cross removed the consequences of that original sin, but not humanity's sinful nature, and, therefore, even Christians are in constant danger of falling into sin and jeopardizing their chance at eternal life. Following the ethical dictates of Jesus is one way of avoiding that danger. However, the only sure way of avoiding the flames of hell and eternal death is to frankly acknowledge one's sinful nature and to sincerely repent of one's sins through the pangs of guilt and shame.

Needless to say, there is much in this Christian picture of humanity that the West has rejected or modified.

Do You Believe in Heaven and Hell?

Belief in life after death still runs relatively high in both Western Europe and the United States. Europeans, however, believe far less in either heaven or hell than do Americans. About 47 percent of all Europeans believe in heaven and 24 percent believe in hell. In the United States, on the other hand, the same poll showed that about 78 percent believed in the existence in heaven while about 48 percent believed in hell. Of course, even with this relatively high belief in hell, it should be pointed out that very few Americans actually thought they would wind up there.

As for heaven, despite the fact that it is still a popular idea in the West, few today have very strong opinions about what it might be like. In the New Testament, both Jesus and Paul talk of heaven as an actual place where the righteous will spend eternity in the presence of God. Paul even claimed to have been caught up to the "third heaven," although he was bound to secrecy about what it was really like.

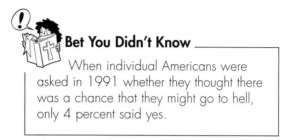

Bet You Didn't Know

When individual Americans were asked in 1991 whether they thought there was a chance that they might go to hell, only 4 percent said yes.

Only in the Book of Revelation do we get a concrete picture of heaven: Here, heaven is pictured as a heavenly copy of the city of Jerusalem, made of crystal, gem stones, and precious metals, and in the middle of which rested the thrones of God and Jesus wrought in green jasper. Inhabiting this city were thousands of angels who perpetually sang the divine praises. Later conceptions of heaven would turn it from the urban to the rural, envisioning it as the Garden of Eden. Here the recently deceased meet with dead loved ones and carry on a life much like an earthly picnic.

While interest in heaven has remained high among Americans, by the 1980s and 1990s, people were loath to describe it, often thinking of it in terms of a permanent psychological state as opposed to a place. Some scholars speculate that modernity, with the rise of scientific cosmology, has made such concrete visions of the afterlife unbelievable. Other scholars point to the rising number of people who believe in reincarnation as another reason for the decline in speculation about the nature of heaven.

Divine Inspiration

Today, nearly a quarter of the population of the West profess a belief in reincarnation. For them, heaven is to be reached only after a seemingly endless series of lifetimes and, as such, is almost too distant to be imagined.

Does Sin Lead to Damnation?

Of all of the core beliefs of Christianity regarding the nature and destiny of humanity, the doctrine of sin has perhaps undergone the most radical transformation in the West. As one commentator has put it, "… the urgent sense of personal sin has all but disappeared in the current upbeat style in American religion." Fewer and fewer people believe in the doctrine of original sin and the idea that children are born sinful is becoming increasingly repugnant to most Westerners.

Most people in the West see unacceptable behavior as the result not of a sinful nature, but due to psychological, sociological, and even biological problems. This tendency to reduce sin to potentially "curable" aspects of human nature means that sin is no longer the occasion for feelings of guilt and shame as it was in the past. Indeed, psychologists today see guilt not as a God-given means of correction for the soul, but as a disabling emotion that needs to be banished from the human psyche.

Perhaps for this reason, the clergy of the main-stream churches in the West no longer emphasize sin and damnation in their sermons and homilies. For the majority of their listeners, such topics have little relevance and are seen to reflect an outdated and—some would say—harmful perspective on the nature of humanity.

Agents from Above: Angels and Devils

One of the great ironies of postmodern Christianity is that, although the West is more comfortable with abstract notions of heaven and denies the reality of sin, a surprising number of people believe in the concrete agents of both: angels and devils.

You're an Angel!

Angels and devils, of course, have had a long history in Christianity. Christianity inherited a strong tradition about such creatures from Judaism, and in the New Testament, angels and devils make frequent appearances. The angel Gabriel, for example, brings Mary the news of her miraculous conception of Jesus, and Jesus himself was opposed throughout his ministry by the chief of devils, Satan himself.

The mythology of angels and devils has subsequently been extremely popular in the West. Since the Enlightenment of the eighteenth century, however, the reality of angels and devils was played down in most official contexts, and, in step with the rationalism of the times, angels and devils became metaphors for good and evil, but not concrete beings, in institutional Christianity. Popular belief in such beings began to wane as well.

At the end of the twentieth century, however, belief in angels and devils as concrete entities has made an amazing comeback. The belief in angels and personal encounters with angels is on the rise in the United States.

In most supermarket tabloids, stories and purported photographs of angels have appeared with even more frequency than stories about UFOs. In addition, angels are prominent characters on television and in Hollywood films. "Experts" on angelology or those who claim to have encountered angels are now sought-after guests for television and radio talk shows. Scores of people are now paying thousands of dollars to participate in "psychotherapy" workshops that sponsors claim will enable people to establish contact with their guardian angels in order to facilitate personal growth.

Many have speculated on the roots of this angel craze, and cite the fact that it is essentially non-denominational in character as part of its allure. Despite the fact that most of the details of modern angelology are taken from Roman Catholicism, the majority of people interested in angels see them as simply spiritual beings that have no intrinsic connection to any Christian denomination. Many cite their knowledge that angels are found in other world religions as proof that they are essentially non-Christian in character.

> **Bet You Didn't Know**
>
> Popular books about angels have remained on the best-seller lists for months, and have become a mass-market phenomenon. Magazines devoted to angels have sprung up, as have websites.

The Devil Made Me Do It

The craze for benevolent angels began in the early 1990s. Almost a decade and a half earlier, another wave of fascination swept over the West, and this time it involved not angels but devils.

Up to that point, belief in the Devil as a personal agent of evil had been declining in the modern West. The old Christian stereotype of Satan as a horned monster was out of place in a world of optimistic rationality. However, after two world wars, countless mechanized massacres, and a host of other evils of the modern world, Satan no longer seemed so far-fetched. This was especially true in America, where fascination with Satan reached new highs.

By the 1980s, a kind of "Satanic panic" gripped the United States, with special police squads being formed to investigate the numerous reports of violent Satanic worship throughout the country. While actual Satanism proved hard to find in America, and while belief in Satan has subsequently dropped in the United States, interest in Satanic themes in the popular culture nevertheless still remains high.

Bet You Didn't Know

In response to the high level of Americans' fascination with Satan, there appeared a wave of popular media with Satanic themes. From *Rosemary's Baby* in 1968, to *The Exorcist* in 1973, to *The Omen* in 1976, Satanic possession became a mainstay of American film.

The Least You Need to Know

- The general trend toward the conscious blending of premodern and modern worldviews are considered "postmodern," and therefore the religious balancing act we are witnessing in today's society can properly be called "postmodern" Christianity.

- While people still believe that religion is an important part of life, people also feel that one should determine one's own religious beliefs independent of organized religion.

- In the United States, about 78 percent believe in the existence in heaven while about 48 percent believe in hell; though, only very few Americans actually thought they would wind up there.

- Most people in the West see unacceptable behavior as the result of psychological, sociological, and even biological problems, not of a sinful nature.

- Although the West is more comfortable with abstract notions of heaven and denies the reality of sin, a surprising number of people believe in the concrete agents of both angels and devils.

Chapter 9

Christian Practice in a Postmodern Age

In This Chapter

- Church service, prayers, and holidays
- Pilgrimage shrines
- Spiritual healing
- Christianity's future

Postmodern Christianity is by its very nature a plural phenomenon: There is no *one* postmodern Christian tradition. In this chapter, we will attempt to come to terms with postmodern Christianity in the West by contrasting a wide range of postmodern practices with those "official" practices espoused by the institutional churches. As we do so, we shall also explore how the tensions between postmodern and official practices (as well as the beliefs from Chapter 8) are slowly transforming the Christian tradition as a whole.

Postmodern Christian Practices

Throughout this book, we have charted the continuing evolution of Christian practice, from the very simple rituals of baptism and Eucharist of the early Church to the complex liturgies developed by the churches in the Middle Ages and the Reformation. During this period, the whole of Christian life was structured such that every day, week, year, and even the human life cycle itself (birth, marriage, death), was regularly punctuated with periods of sacred time. Today, this evolution continues, but at an accelerated pace.

In postmodern Christianity, many of the most important Christian practices are being rejected or simply ignored, some are being modified or blended with non-Christian practices, and, in some cases, practices from Christianity's past long ignored by some segments of Christianity are being rediscovered and renewed.

Did You Attend Church Service This Week?

In the West, participation in Sunday services and knowledge of the sacraments has fallen off sharply. Indeed, it can be safely said that the Eucharist is no longer the sacramental center of most Western Christians' lives, whether Catholic or Protestant, and with the de-emphasis of sin in the West, confession and penance are now largely a thing of the past. And yet, the majority of Americans and Europeans still resort to the churches to mediate significant points in the life cycle: birth (baptism), adulthood (marriage), and death (funeral rites).

In the Roman Catholic and Anglican tradition, this has led to the phenomenon of the so-called "service churches," that is, churches where a majority of the congregation only attend rites of passage, much to the irritation of the clergy. In some cases, parish priests have threatened to withhold services to those who do not attend services on a regular basis, but this has only served to drive people away even from church-mediated life-cycle rituals.

If Sabbath attendance is down, individual practice is up. According to recent surveys, when asked to reconcile the fact that most Americans say they are highly religious with the fact that they do not attend services, many said that it was because they pre-ferred to worship in private than to worship in public. Perhaps for this reason, prayer is making a comeback in the West.

On the Right Path

The return to prayer has had a sig-nificant impact on the popular culture in America as well. Today, more than 2,000 titles on prayer can be found in *Books in Print,* and more than 1,000 ecumenical prayer workshops have sprung up around the United States. Many are organized and run by lay people, and some prayer workshops are promoted as ways in which individuals can design personal "prayer programs" using elements from Christian mysticism, Hindu yoga, and Buddhist meditation techniques.

Did You Say Your Prayers?

By far the most democratic of all Christian practices, prayer is seen as the means by which an individual places him- or herself in direct contact with God, either to give thanks, to ask a favor, or simply to experience God's presence. For most Christians, therefore, prayer provides a sense of security and comfort, and, for some Christians, prayer is the source of the most intense and satisfying experiences of their religious life.

Inherited from earlier Jewish practice, Christian prayer is specifically enjoined in the Gospels. In Matthew and Luke, Jesus taught a short prayer (the "Lord's Prayer") to his disciples that acknowledged the sovereignty of God, asked his forgiveness, and sought his continued favor in the necessities of life. It is precisely the simplicity and privacy of prayer that seems to attract large numbers of Western Christians today.

Prayer is less popular in Western Europe, with fewer than a quarter of all Europeans practicing regular prayer. Recently, however, a worldwide prayer movement based in France has become increasingly popular, not only in the rest of Europe, but also in Japan, India, and the United States as well.

Called Taizé after the village in eastern France where it originated in the 1940s, the goal of the movement is to promote nondenominational group prayer as an effort to reinvigorate spirituality in general. Taizé prayer practices include silent meditation, the singing of improvised hymns, songs, and Gregorian chant, the burning of candles and incense, and, in some case, the chanting of Hindu-style mantras. Structured around a central monastic organization consisting today of 110 monks from a variety of Christian denominations, Taizé encourages the formation of local "cell groups" in which Taizé-style prayer can be carried on locally.

Divine Inspiration

Although the Taizé movement is rigorously nondenominational, it has enjoyed the approbation of such religious leaders as Pope John Paul II and the Archbishop of Canterbury, George Carey.

In addition, it is claimed that every year tens of thousands of people from around the world make the pilgrimage to Taizé to spend a week in communal prayer. During the 1990s, international Taizé meetings have been held in cities around the world, with the Paris meeting in 1994 attracting an estimated 110,000 people for five days of prayer.

Religious Holiday or Vacation Day?

The same kind of Western ambivalence to institutionalized worship can be found for the Christian ritual year. Some Christian festivals remain highly popular (Christmas and Easter), while others are all but forgotten (Good Friday).

In 1997, for example, 96 percent of all Americans celebrated Christmas in some form, and a majority of Americans still observe Easter. For most, however, these are family holidays, with only half of all Americans attending church services on Easter, ostensibly the most important feast day in the Christian calendar.

Nevertheless, on the positive side, surveys have shown that what little knowledge people have about the Bible and Christian doctrine is largely associated with these two holidays. There is also an enduring willingness on the part of state and local governments in the United States to protect the official status of these holidays, and this is despite the growing religious pluralism of the United States.

The same cannot be said of other Christian holidays: Recently, in response to a class-action lawsuit, a state-mandated Good Friday holiday for the Illinois school system was struck down as unconstitutional since, in the words of one judge, the official celebrating of Good Friday "conveys the impermissible message that Christianity is a favored religion." So far, similar challenges to the far more popular festivals of Christmas and Easter have failed.

In the face of falling interest in Christian holidays, some churches have begun to explore new festivals that might have more relevance to their constituencies. Some African American churches, for example, have adopted *Kwanzaa* as a Christian holiday. Kwanzaa is observed from December 26 to January 1, and celebrates the seven cardinal principles of unity, self-determination, collective labor and responsibility, cooperative economics, purpose, creativity, and faith.

As Kwanzaa has become increasingly popular, some African-American churches have sought to integrate Kwanzaa into their liturgies. The Faith United

Methodist Church in Los Angeles now holds special "See Christ in Kwanzaa" services during the Kwanzaa season, and its pastor encourages his congregation to celebrate the special seven-night Kwanzaa candle-lighting ceremony with their families at home. Many other African-American denominations are following suit.

Spread the Word _____

Kwanzaa, a Swahili word meaning "first fruits of the harvest," was established in 1966 by a black social activist named Maulana Ron Karenga. Karenga wished Kwanzaa to be an opportunity for blacks to rediscover their cultural roots.

Pilgrimage on the Rise

Although participation in the sacraments is down, the sacramental urge has not completely disappeared in the West. In Europe, for example, the attendance at pilgrimage shrines is way up. In 1992, the shrine at Lourdes in France had a record 5.5 million visitors, representing a 1.5 million increase over 10 years. Other pilgrimage destinations, such as Santiago de Compostela in Spain and Fatima in Portugal, report similar increases. Many come for the healing miracles reported at such places, but others come simply to be in the presence of the divine, something which many say they no longer feel at their local churches.

On the Right Path

For the first time since the 1500s, the relics belonging to St. Thomas à Becket (d. 1170) have been placed on display in Canterbury Cathedral. Canterbury was one of the most popular pilgrimage shrines in Europe, attracting thousands until it was suppressed by Henry VIII. Some within the Anglican Church felt that reinstallation of the relics would violate the spirit of the Reformation, but church authorities claimed they were simply responding to overwhelming public interest in reestablishing an historic pilgrimage.

What is truly interesting, however, is that not all the people flocking to these Catholic shrines are Catholics. Large numbers of Protestants also mingle with the Catholic pilgrims and attend Catholic services at the shrines. Despite a ban on pilgrimage dating from the Reformation, Protestants in Europe are finding in Catholic pilgrimage satisfaction of their need to be in the presence of the holy. Indeed, some Protestant denominations, notably the Anglican Church, are taking note.

Since the United States through much of its history was predominantly Protestant, no pilgrimage tradition developed. The Catholic Church does sponsor some pilgrimage shrines in the United States, but most of these sites do not seem to attract the same kind of Protestant crossover that similar shrines do in Europe. A growing number of people, however, both Protestant and Catholic, churched and unchurched, have been attracted to Pentecostal services. In a sense, the attraction of such services is sacramental: the promise of experiencing God's direct contact through the Holy Spirit.

Indeed, one such Pentecostal church has developed into a de facto pilgrimage. Since 1995, the Brownsville Assembly of God in Pensacola, Florida, has been attracting some 3,000 to 6,000 people a night. Some come from as far away as Australia, the Ukraine, Japan, and Zimbabwe, all hoping for a chance to participate in the evening services led by a charismatic Pentecostal preacher named Steve Hill.

By noon every day, hundreds of people form themselves into a line that stretches for a city block from the front door of the church. Why do people wait for hours to get inside? Many believe with absolute conviction that, despite its mundane appearance, the Holy Spirit can be encountered there. "This is the place God has chosen," said one pilgrim. "He's here." And as if in confirmation of this claim, every night hundreds of people weep, shout, jerk uncontrollably, dance in the aisles, or simply faint dead away at the touch of the preacher's hand on their forehead. By May 1997, some 107,000 had claimed to have experienced God in the Brownsville church, making this, the so-called "Pensacola Outpouring," not only the longest continuously running revival in American history, but also one of the most successful.

Satisfy Your Urges Through Spiritual Healing

Another way in which the sacramental urge is satisfied in the postmodern West is through spiritual healing, including Christian healing. Throughout the history of Christianity, the belief that divine power can be used to cure weakness or disease of the body has been a powerful one. The Gospels abound with examples of Jesus curing physical and psychological disease, and one of the arguments for his divinity has always been his power to heal.

Indeed, healing has always remained an important function of the Christian churches. According to the Apostle Paul, those who had the power to heal were to be ranked alongside those who could preach, prophesy, and speak in tongues. Even non-Christians began to seek the help of churches for healing, and there is evidence that certain "freelance" healers roamed the Greco-Roman world, claiming to cure disease simply by invoking the name of Jesus. The medieval Catholic Church institutionalized spiritual healing through the sacrament of the Anointing of the Sick (also known as Extreme Unction).

With the rise of modernity and medical science, belief in spiritual healing declined in the West. Some Christian denominations did make spiritual healing a cornerstone in their theology (Christian Science), but for most Christians it played a decreasingly important part of their faith.

In the last decades of the twentieth century, however, there has been a small renaissance of spiritual healing, of both Christian and non-Christian forms. Impatient with conventional therapies, many people are turning to "alternative" treatments to relieve psychological suffering and organic disease. To a limited extent, even the medical establishment has begun to reassess the effectiveness of spiritual healing as a form of "complementary care."

As might be expected, in this environment there is also a rise in the number of people seeking specifically Christian healing. In response, the Catholic Church has reemphasized the importance of Extreme Unction, which, despite its popular name of "last rites," is actually a general sacrament for physical healing that can be sought by anyone who is seriously ill. To this end, since Vatican II, the sacrament has been referred to simply as Anointing of the Sick.

Bet You Didn't Know

Cancer centers around the nation now include such things as New Age therapeutic touch, yoga, acupressure—even the Japanese Tea Ceremony.

A number of denominations have also developed health-care systems that seek to integrate Christian practice with modern medical care. There are limits to the acceptance of spiritual healing, though.

More and more parents who opt exclusively for spiritual healing for their children have been prosecuted for neglect, and in cases where children have died while under the care of faith healers, parents have been sentenced to jail.

Where Will Christianity Go?

The West's ambivalent attitude toward spiritual healing is a perfect example of the postmodern desire to balance modern and premodern beliefs and practices. On the one hand, the West is a long way from abandoning its faith in science and rationalism; on the other hand, most Westerners have realized that science and rationalism alone cannot provide all the answers.

Bet You Didn't Know

In one case where the parents were prosecuted for neglect in Minnesota, a jury levied a $14 million verdict against the Christian Science Church, stating that they hoped the size of the award would "send a message" to Christian Scientists and other believers in spiritual healing.

To a certain degree, this has meant a return to Christianity, although not a return to institutional Christianity. Faith in the West is now constructed through a dynamic balancing of modern and premodern elements, and this is something the institutional churches, with their historic concern for a rigidly defined orthodoxy, are not in a position to do. In turn, this has led to the creation of what we have been calling postmodern Christianity: a highly private affair in which the believer feels entitled to create and recreate the mix of modernity with Christian premodernity that best satisfies his or her spiritual needs.

Another mark of postmodern Christianity is its open syncretism (the combining of different forms of belief and practice). As we have seen in this book, the history of Christianity can be seen largely as a history of syncretism. However, in contrast to the past, many Western Christians pursue syncretism today openly and without apology.

The majority of people in the West now feel that the churches no longer give adequate answers to all of humanity's spiritual questions. This has led to the conviction that it is important to explore religious paths other than Christianity. Christians in the West have thus begun to demonstrate a lively interest in other world religions, such as Hinduism, Buddhism, Islam, and so on.

Many Christians are now uncomfortable with claims of the uniqueness of Christianity, and many more profess to believe that all religions are equal. Indeed, in the face of modernity, one way in which Westerners have sought to "prove" certain Christian beliefs and doctrines is to find their analogs in other world religions. The more that Christian beliefs can be "translated" into the beliefs and symbols of other traditions, it is believed, the higher the probability that they are true.

What then is the future of Christianity in the West? Mainstream Christian institutions are, of course, reluctant to sanction the kind of religious translation or the syncretism that postmodernism encourages. Nor can they endure the kind of rapid reassessment and perpetual mixing and compromising that postmodern Christians require. Does this mean the permanent eclipse of institutional Christianity in the West? Perhaps. Christianity, after all, is a living tradition.

Throughout its history, Christianity has constantly changed and metamorphosed to meet the challenges of new ages. And just as early Christians could hardly have predicted the shape of medieval or modern Christianity, so, too, it is impossible for us to predict with any accuracy the ultimate shape that Christianity might take in a postmodern age.

The Least You Need to Know

- According to recent surveys, when asked to reconcile the fact that most Americans say they are highly religious with the fact that they do not attend services, many said that it was because they preferred to worship in private than to worship in public.

- For most Christians, therefore, prayer provides a sense of security and comfort, and, for some Christians, prayer is the source of the most intense and satisfying experiences of their religious life.

- Some Christian festivals remain highly popular (Christmas and Easter), others are all but forgotten (Good Friday), while new ones (Kwanzaa) are gaining popularity.

- Although participation in the sacraments is down, the sacramental urge has not completely disappeared in the West through increased attendance at pilgrimage shrines.

- Spiritual healing satisfies the sacramental urge for some Christians, while with the rise of modernity and medical science, belief in spiritual healing is on the decline.

- Throughout its history, Christianity has constantly changed and metamorphosed to meet the challenges of new ages.

Glossary

agape   A communal meal that was commonly celebrated by early Christians as part of the Eucharist.

apocalypticism   The belief in the imminent end of the world; in Christianity this belief is coupled with the expectation of the Second Coming of Jesus (see also *Millennialism*).

apologists, apology   A group of theologians from the Ancient period who sought to reinterpret the Christian message in light of Greek philosophy.

apostle   Specifically, "apostle" refers to one of the followers of Jesus who was chosen to preach the Gospel; generally, it refers to any person who engages in a Christian mission.

atonement   The reconciliation of God with humankind.

baptism   The Christian ritual of initiation by which a person is spiritually purified through contact with water. The practice was adopted by Christians in imitation of Jesus' baptism by John at the River Jordan, as depicted in the Gospels.

bishop   In the Roman Catholic, Eastern Orthodox, Anglican, and other Episcopal Churches, bishops are high-ranking officials, responsible for a diocese.

canon   A fixed list of documents considered divinely inspired.

catechumens   In the early Church, catechumens were persons in training for admission to the Church. Unbaptized, the catechumens were only allowed to witness the first part of the Mass and were dismissed before the Eucharist.

confirmation Sacrament administered by a bishop by means of which baptized persons are admitted to full Church membership in such traditions as Roman Catholicism or Eastern Orthodoxy. The rite includes laying on of hands and anointing with oil. In the Eastern Orthodox Churches, confirmation follows the baptism of an infant, while in the Roman Catholic Church it is administered when a child reaches the age of reason.

covenant A bond sealed between God and the Jews by which the Jews are promised God's favor in exchange for their fidelity. Christians believe that because of the sacrifice of Jesus they are successors to the Jews in this bond.

creed A set of doctrinal statements that attempts to summarize the Christian faith and define Orthodoxy.

crusade Literally "warfare on behalf of the cross," crusades were military expeditions sanctioned by the papacy.

deacon One of the earliest of the Church offices, deacons were responsible for assisting priests at Mass, instructing catechumens, and administering charity.

denominationalism The separation of Christian tradition into a number of autonomous voluntary organizations.

ecumenicism An ongoing movement that encourages the worldwide reunion and cooperation of the Christian churches.

Eucharist The sacrament of consecrated bread and wine, recreating the last meal partaken by Jesus with his disciples before his crucifixion.

Evangelical Protestantism A broad movement that developed within Protestantism in the eighteenth century, which emphasizes a democratic style of preaching, millennialism, and pietism.

excommunicate To expel from Church membership.

Extreme Unction (also known as Last Rites or Sacrament for the Sick) In Roman Catholicism, a sacrament intended to facilitate physical healing or to ease death in sick or dying individuals.

fundamentalism Fundamentalism is not a single denomination, but a set of beliefs and attitudes that cut across denominational boundaries. Fundamentalists stress five basic points: (1) the inerrancy of Scripture; (2) the virgin birth of Jesus; (3) atonement limited to the elect; (4) the physical, bodily resurrection of Jesus; and (5) the literal Second Coming of Jesus.

gnosticism A form of Christianity from Late Antiquity. Gnostics believed that Jesus had brought secret knowledge (gnosis) necessary for salvation. Part of this gnosis was the sharp division between matter (which was evil) and spirit (which was good).

Gospels Meaning "good news," the Gospels are narratives about the life of Jesus and his message.

grace In Christian theology, God's love and assistance freely given to Christian believers without which salvation would not be possible.

Hebrew Bible The sacred scriptures of the Jews (called the Old Testament by Christians).

heresy Doctrines and beliefs that depart from orthodox teaching.

Higher Criticism of the Bible The scholarly movement that attempted to separate fact from myth in the Bible by subjugating it to the same kind of scientific analysis used with other historical documents.

Holy Spirit The third person of the Trinity, often thought of as God's guiding presence in the churches.

icons In Eastern Orthodoxy, special pictures of Jesus and Mary, the angels, saints, and martyrs that are believed to have special powers of intercession and protection.

indulgences In Roman Catholic theology, indulgences assure people that by participating in extra devotions, a certain portion of their future stay in purgatory will be remitted and their entrance into heaven hastened.

Inquisition An ecclesiastical court set up by the Catholic Church in the Middle Ages to root out heresy.

justification In Christian theology, the reconciliation of one's will with the will of God, leading to salvation.

Kingdom of God The rule of God on earth, which Christians believe is now manifested in the churches, but which will ultimately be universal at the end of time.

Liberation Theology A twentieth-century theological movement within Roman Catholicism. According to Liberation Theology, sin is the result not only of personal failings, but of social inequalities. Catholics, therefore, are obligated to fight for social justice as much as they are obligated to fight against personal sin.

liturgy   The form and content of public worship in the Christian churches.

mainstream Christianity   The denomination (or denominations) to which the majority of people within a country or region adhere.

marriage   The sacrament by which Christian churches hallow relationships between men and women.

martyr   A Christian who dies for the faith.

Mass   The weekly Christian ritual in which the Eucharist is celebrated.

messiah   A future king from the line of David whom the Jews believe will eventually appear to restore Israel. Christians believe that Jesus was the Messiah, and the title Christos is Greek for "anointed one."

millennialism   The Christian belief that the Last Judgment will be preceded by Jesus' Second Coming to earth and of his establishment of a thousand years of peace and prosperity—the millennium.

modernists   Christians who see the products of science as providing new and exciting ways to approach the Christian faith.

modernity   Represented a peculiarly new world-view in human history. It emphasized skepticism and critical thinking, as well as a positive attitude toward social and intellectual change. Modernity also tended to de-emphasize the importance of the transcendent in the world, and insisted on the paramount role of the individual in shaping the future.

monastery   A dwelling place where either monks or nuns live according to monastic rule.

monasticism, monk   Monks are people who seek to live a more pure Christian life by withdrawing from society and the sensual world, in order to pursue an ordered life of contemplation, known as monasticism.

mysticism   Practices that bring an individual into the immediate presence of God.

ordination   Rituals by which individuals are admitted to the priesthood or ministry.

orthodoxy   Correct belief as defined by the majority Church.

orthopraxy   Correct practice as defined by the majority Church.

Passover   In Judaism, the annual celebration of the Ancient Hebrews' escape from slavery in Egypt.

patriarch   Tribal head in the era before Moses; also, the title of the leaders of the national churches in Eastern Orthodox Christianity.

pentecostalism   A religious movement within Protestantism that began in the United States in the early twentieth century. It emphasized spontaneous participation in worship and immediate experience of the Holy Spirit.

pietism   Protestant movements that sought to place the nonrational and experimental elements of the tradition above overly rationalized doctrinal elements.

postmodernity   The current period of Western history characterized by a blending of premodern and modern worldviews.

predestination   In Christian theology, the belief that God has foreordained an individual's salvation or damnation from the beginning of time.

presbyter   In the early Church, presbyters were a body of elders who aided bishops.

priest   In the Roman Catholic, Eastern Orthodox, Anglican, and other Episcopal Churches, priests are the mid-level clergymen responsible for a parish.

prophet   Religious reformers who legitimate their reformist goals by claiming to speak to God.

Protestants   Those denominations that arose in response to the Reformation.

purgatory   In Roman Catholic theology, a destination where the dead are purified to their earthly sins through suffering, in preparation for admission to heaven.

relics   The earthly remains and other objects associated with Christian martyrs and saints; such objects are seen as containing a superabundance of spiritual power.

resurrection   Reanimation of the body after death.

revivalism, revivals   Large-scale movements of religious enthusiasm, sometimes lasting for months or years.

sacrament   A physical act that leads to direct and immediate contact with divine grace.

saints   In Roman Catholic and Eastern Orthodox theology, extraordinary Christians who, upon death, are worthy of veneration and who can intercede for believers on earth.

salvation   The achievement of eternal life.

scholasticism   The medieval intellectual movement that developed in the universities of Europe during the twelfth century. Scholasticism was characterized by a rigorous use of logic to reconcile reason with faith, and to discern the limits of both.

syncretism   The conscious or unconscious blending of elements from two distinct religious traditions.

Trinity   The Christian doctrine that defines divinity as an identity between God, Jesus, and the Holy Spirit.

Index

D

E